Happy Birthday Katie

Winnie and Harry

CLASSICS

the best the world has to offer

By Mon Muellerschoen and Peter Steinfeld

General Publishing Group
Los Angeles

Publisher: W. Quay Hays
Editorial Director: Peter L. Hoffman
Art Director: Chitra Sekhar
Production Director: Trudihope Schlomowitz
Prepress Manager: Bill Castillo
Production Assistants: Tom Archibeque, Lisa Barnes, David Chadderdon, Gus Dawson, Gaston Moraga,
  Phillis Stacy, Regina Troyer
Editorial Assistant: Dana Stibor
Copy Editor: Dianne Woo

For information:
General Publishing Group, Inc.
2701 Ocean Park Boulevard, Suite 140
Santa Monica, CA 90405

Library of Congress Cataloging-in-Publication Data

Muellerschoen, Mon.
    Classics : the best the world has to offer / by Mon Muellerschoen and Peter Steinfeld.
        p.   cm.
    ISBN 1-57544-030-X (hardcover)
    1. Popular culture--United States--History--20th century-
    -Dictionaries. 2. Popular culture--History--20th century-
    -Dictionaries. 3. Consumer goods--United States--History--20th
    century--Dictionaries. 4. Consumer goods--History--20th century-
    -Dictionaries. I. Steinfeld, Peter. II. Title.
    E169.04.M79 1997
    306'.0973--dc21   97-22588
                                                                              CIP

Printed in the USA
10 9 8 7 6 5 4 3 2 1

General Publishing Group
Los Angeles

To my beloved sons, Linus and Lukas.

—Mon Muellerschoen

CLASSICS Contents

ABEL AUTOMATICS

What comes to most people's minds when they hear the term *fly fishing* is elderly men waist high in a lazy stream, clad in rubber waders. Not exactly living on the edge.

But then maybe that's what has made Abel Automatics founder Steve Abel so cutting edge in the hitherto gentle art of angling. The simple act of tying a fly onto a line wound onto an Abel reel has somehow become the equivalent of strapping a snowboard to your feet and hitting a double diamond trail.

When he was a young adult, Steve made his living as a professional deep-sea diver who helped remove sunken ships from the Suez Canal. By 1976, he gave up his full-time days in the deep and opened up a shop that put his machinist skills to good use.

Focusing his efforts on fashioning high-tech parts for military and aerospace projects, Steve's ingenuity soon found its way into nearly every Boeing aircraft in operation.

While this work proved rewarding, it lacked the certain communing-with-nature quality he'd experienced as a

boy fishing off the piers in Oceanside, California, just up the road from San Diego.

In the mid-1980s, the idea of returning to his pescatory roots finally lured Steve away from the daily grind. Relying on his machinist expertise, he purchased many of the leading fly reels on the market and pulled them apart to see what made them work and how they might work better.

Taking into account the extreme weather conditions that fly fishermen endure, Steve fashioned his first Abel reel in March of 1988. Later that year, his hard work earned him the much-coveted Kudo Award from *Fly Rod & Reel* magazine. Abel reels were an instant success and well on their way to classic stature.

Although his award-winning reel was ideal for catching trout, Steve had bigger fish to fry. He began designing reels that could withstand the rigors of saltwater big game fish. Not too surprisingly, he was successful.

By 1996, Abel reels had set 61 International Game Fish Association (IGFA) records, including a 140-pound blue shark, a 72-pound mako shark, and a 67-pound wahoo, all caught by Abel himself.

ALPHA FLIGHT JACKETS

*T*om Cruise is Pete "Maverick" Mitchell. He struts up to Kelly McGillis' doorstep after having played volleyball on the beach with Goose, Slider, and Ice Man. Pete's dressed in true Top Gun style: wearing his government-issued mirrored shades, jeans, a white T-shirt, and the final pièce de résistance, a CWU-45/P flight jacket.

The T-shirt? You can get it at any Gap outlet. The jeans? Same place, different aisle. The mirrored shades? In Los Angeles, you can get 'em for four bucks on Venice Beach, or for six bucks in Astor Place in New York. The flight jacket? This item can be purchased only through Alpha Industries, Inc., "original and genuine" supplier to the U.S. military forces for nearly 40 years.

Opening their Knoxville, Tennessee, doors in 1959, the company began with humble aspirations. They made cold-weather apparel: jackets, parkas, caps.

ALPHA USA

Aviation breakthroughs were rendering leather fleece-lined bomber jackets impractical. It was the late 1940s, and the jet age created a need for new flight jackets. As the flight deck was raised drastically, those classic bomber jackets left pilots shivering in their boots.

Unheard-of elevations exposed pilots to new levels of frigidity. And what was worse, the fleece lining not only retained moisture but also froze as planes reached higher altitudes. In addition, streamlined cockpits were making it difficult for pilots to move in bulky leather outerwear.

The armed forces began experimenting with nylon. This material had been proposed earlier in the World War II effort, but resources were low and parachutes consumed the majority of the supply; any residual nylon generally went to the wives of high-ranking officials. But by 1944, the need for an improved flight jacket could no longer be ignored.

First up was the B-15, which met with some success and popularity, but would last for only five years before being replaced by the classic MA-1 flight jacket. Issued to U.S. Air Force and Navy pilots, these jackets had a nylon shell with a nylon lining and a wool interlining.

Over the course of the next several years, the jackets became so popular that they were being sold on the European black market. Then, in 1958, Alpha Industries got their first contract to produce the MA-1 for the armed forces.

They made several alterations, such as replacing the wool interlining with a polyester fiberfill and doing away with the mouton fur collar because it interfered with aviators' parachute harnesses. Obviously the new style was a huge success, for now, 39 years later, Alpha Industries has become the "preferred choice of professional military forces throughout the world."

JACKET, FLYING, MAN'S,
INTERMEDIATE, MA-1
MIL-J-8279D (USAF)   SIZE MEDIUM
8415-818-7352
DSA-1-4249-64-C   6 MAY 1964
ALPHA INDUSTRIES, Inc.
INTERLINING: 58% WOOL, 42% COTTON
DRY CLEAN ONLY

ALPHA INDUSTRIES INC
B-15 FLIGHT JACKET
Marilyn Monroe, Korean Tour, 1954

AMERICAN EXPRESS

*R*egardless of where one may be in the world, whether it's a thriving Manhattanesque metropolis or a Masai tribal hut nestled in the expanse of the Great Rift Valley, there's bound to be an American Express office nearby.

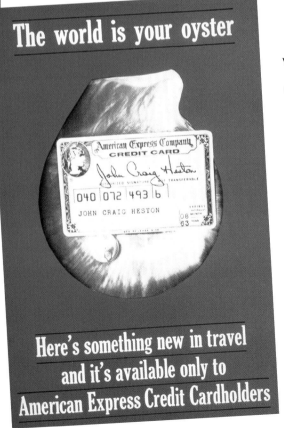

The world is your oyster

Here's something new in travel and it's available only to American Express Credit Cardholders

The route to this ubiquitous presence traces back to 1841, when Henry Wells started a company specializing in the transporting of valuables. Not long after, Wells teamed up with a gentleman by the name of William G. Fargo.

The two men expanded into money orders and traveler's checks and, after a split in 1846, reunited with competitor John Butterfield. This new partnership, formed on March 18, 1850, was called the American Express Company.

From that moment on, the company solidified their place in American mercantilism through freight shipping, railroad contract negotiating, and transcontinental mail service. This last venture won them the first U.S. Postal Service mail contract, which, of course, led to their involvement in the pony express, servicing the West from 1860 to 1861.

Yet, despite such business innovations and industry breakthroughs, American Express has become most closely associated with something that Wells, Fargo, and Butterfield had never envisioned: the American Express card....Don't leave home without it.™

It was Diners Club who introduced the idea of credit cards to the country in the 1950s. American Express was intrigued by the concept but feared that following suit might render their lucrative traveler's check business obsolete. Company president Ralph T. Reed objected to the proposal of instituting such a service but wisely came around and, in 1958, the first American Express travel-and-entertainment card was launched.

The soon-to-be-famous credit card was actually purple and made of cardboard, a far cry from the green plastic we've come to know and owe. In fact, on Day 1 of its release, 300,000 people tendered applications. Three months later, it could claim more than 500,000 members and, by the end of 1959, the card accounted for nearly $59 million in earnings.

The first gold card was launched in 1966, and the introduction of the green card ended the purple reign just three years later. It would be yet another four years before the first card with a magnetic strip would be issued.

Since then, plenty of us have been denied the 1984 Platinum Card, the 1987 Optima Card, and the 1994 Rewards Plus Gold Card. The American Express membership miles program, which gives subscribers one mile for every dollar spent, was quite a benefit for art collector Eli Broad, who purchased Roy Lichtenstein's *I'm Sorry* at a Sotheby's sale for $2.5 million—the highest-priced single purchase ever charged on the card.

Today, there are nearly 40 million American Express cards in circulation.

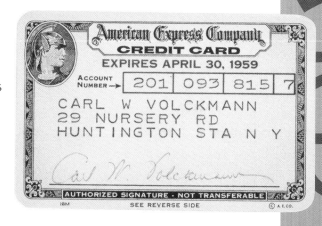

CREDIT CARDS

BARBIE®

Who is the most prolific

designer of women's apparel?

Is it Isaac Mizrahi? Or perhaps

Donna Karan? What about Oscar de la Renta? No, the actual leader in haute

couter, with a shocking one billion fashions is...Mattel, the

creators of the Barbie® doll and her friends.

Since her debut in 1959, Barbie has left Imelda Marcos in the dust with no less than one billion shoes. Then there are the fashionable outfits cut from more than 125 million yards of fabric.

How did this phenomenon come to exist? Well, many times, Ruth Handler, co-founder of Mattel, witnessed her young daughter, Barbara, playing with adult paper dolls.

Ruth met with her design staff. She tried to convince them to three-dimensionalize the paper doll, to make real dolls and accessories that girls could play with in the same way. The idea was met with considerable skepticism. But Ruth persevered, and after several years and several designs the original Barbie® doll hit the 1959 New York Toy Fair.

Vendors at the Toy Fair regarded "Teen-Age Fashion Model" Barbie as too risky. "Little girls want to play with baby dolls whom they can diaper and feed," they blathered.

"They want to learn how to grow up to be good mothers and housewives. What's all this future career rubbish?" But Ruth was undaunted. She had vision.

Mattel launched a TV campaign that made the Barbie doll an overnight sensation. And not only that, but little girls wanted a Barbie who did more than just look great in Paris couture. Why couldn't she be a college graduate in 1963? Why couldn't she be an astronaut in 1965? How about a surgeon in 1973? Or a summit diplomat in 1990? And, if Ross Perot could do it, then why couldn't Barbie be a presidential candidate in 1992?

Priced at around $3.00 when first created, the lowest-priced dolls are still only $5.00 or $6.00, with the standard one selling for $10.00. The Barbie circle of friends includes Ken®—her beau since 1961—along with her best friend Midge® and little sister Skipper®. The most recent addition is Share a Smile™ Becky®, who sits in a wheelchair. The Barbie doll is sold in more than 140 countries, and the more than 40 Dolls of the World marketed through the years have included Eskimo Barbie, Russian Barbie, Jamaican Barbie and Native American Barbie.

Now well into her 38th year, the 11$\frac{1}{2}$-inch Barbie has become the most successful fashion doll of all time. If you laid out head-to-toe the nearly one billion Barbie and Her Friends dolls sold, they would encircle the earth over seven times.

13

DOLLS

BARNUM'S ANIMAL CRACKERS

Lions and tigers and bears...oh my! In the late 1800s, America's fascination with intricately designed cookies reached a sweet-toothed pitch. Bakeries far and wide began stocking up on animal-shaped cookies imported from England. Called Animals, these cookies became so coveted that U.S. bakers started making them themselves.

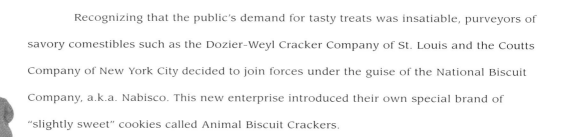

Recognizing that the public's demand for tasty treats was insatiable, purveyors of savory comestibles such as the Dozier-Weyl Cracker Company of St. Louis and the Coutts Company of New York City decided to join forces under the guise of the National Biscuit Company, a.k.a. Nabisco. This new enterprise introduced their own special brand of "slightly sweet" cookies called Animal Biscuit Crackers.

COOKIES

The original Nabisco batches were packaged in the usual large tins or in bulk-type shipments. Sure, the crackers tasted great and the shapes dazzled the eye, but still, there was no overwhelming reason why anyone should choose Nabisco animal crackers over those baked at ye olde neighborhood shoppe.

Then, in 1902, Nabisco marketing geniuses wondered, "Where's the one place to see non-cookie versions of these animals?" Not every town had a zoo, and the only other exposure available to the average citizen was Barnum & Bailey's Circus, which traveled from town to city.

The new name was a hit. That same year, Nabisco sought out strategies for a special Christmas edition. What resulted was packaging that resembled a brightly colored circus wagon displaying drawings of animals. Affixed was the now-famous string handle, which was originally intended as a way to hang the carton from the Christmas tree. For five cents a box, they were sure to please.

Since that auspicious day, Barnum's Animal Crackers have thrilled millions of children the world over. And, while the recipe remains unchanged, the same cannot be said of the original selection of animals. Gone are the days of the jaguar-shaped cookie and the not-so-popular dog cracker.

However, you'll be happy to know that in addition to the lion, tiger, and bear, the current lineup is: cougar, camel, rhino, hippo, kangaroo, hyena, bison, zebra, elephant, sheep, gorilla, monkey, seal, and giraffe.

BASS WEEJUNS

*W*hen G.H. Bass founded his company in 1876, he had no great vision of someday seeing his shoes on the feet of a young man moonwalking across a stage in front of millions, singing "Beat It." Contrary to popular opinion, Bass Weejuns devotee Michael Jackson was not in the original company marketing plan.

Bass

SHOE MAKERS TO AMERICA SINCE 1876

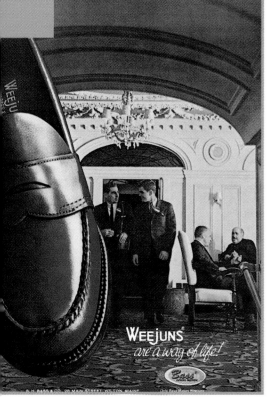

Weejuns
are a way of life!

Setting up shop in Wilton, Maine, George Henry Bass simply wanted to produce a durable line of boots for lumbermen and farmers in his native New England. His utilitarian slogan: "The best possible shoe for the purpose for which it will be used." And with that, he put his tanning expertise to good use and created his first line of hand-sewn shoes.

During the next several years, G.H. Bass & Company enjoyed modest success. Business turned a handsome profit, but to strive for greater wealth was not exactly in keeping with Yankee decorum. The company did proudly design boots worn by Charles Lindbergh on his historic flight in 1927. They also constructed the special boots worn by Admiral Byrd on his second and third Antarctic expeditions. Yet, neither design would be the shoe that put them on the map.

PENNY LOAFERS

It was in the mid-1930s that an *Esquire* magazine editor showed the Bass boys a shoe he'd purchased in Norway. It was part moccasin, part loafer. Bass promptly contacted the shoe's manufacturer and purchased the rights to develop a similar style.

Paying tribute to the shoe's Norwegian origins, the company introduced the Bass Weejun in 1936. The first recorded shipment went to the Rogers Peet company that same year and, soon after, the shoe was offered in their catalog for a shocking $4 a pair. In the ensuing years, Weejun Penny Loafers won a number of admirers, but it wasn't until the mid-1950s, when James Dean donned a pair, that a fashion trend began to brew. Sales increased courtesy of teen rebels feeling the need to wear the same loafers in order to express their deepest angst.

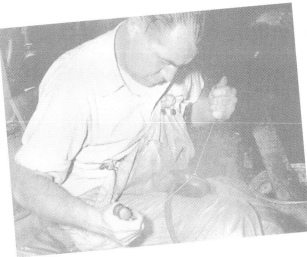

Not until 1960, however, did sales skyrocket, when the *Daily Tar Heel*, the University of North Carolina at Chapel Hill paper, proclaimed that people who wore Bass Weejuns were "with it." The country went wild!

Fashion-forward collegians raced to their nearest retailers, who, sadly, were running out of stock. Did this deter determined trend followers? Absolutely not. Rather, they made pilgrimages to the Wilton, Maine, factory in hopes of snagging a pair hot off the assembly line.

By 1967, Bass was manufacturing and selling over 1.2 million pairs each year. Now, 60 years after their introduction, those same hand-sewn Weejuns that retailed for $4 in 1936 cost roughly $70 and account for over $50 million in sales annually.

WEEJUNS
are a way of life!

G. H. BASS & CO., 46 MAIN STREET, WILTON, MAINE   Only Bass Makes Weejuns

BAYER ASPIRIN

The story of aspirin dates back thousands and thousands of years. In fact, had primitive man known how to market the willow tree parts he chewed to reduce fever, he might've stuck around a little longer than, say, the Paleolithic Era.

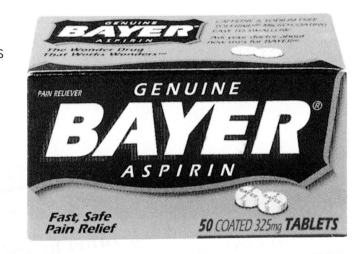

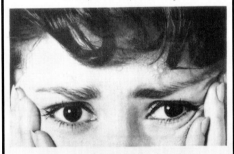

Do you feel "HEAT BEAT"?
...tense, irritable, headachy?

Take a "BAYER BREAK"!

1 Take 2 Bayer Aspirin for your headache. 2 Sit down and relax.

3 With Bayer Aspirin and a few minutes' rest, you'll feel fine in practically no time. Try it.

When the hot weather and high humidity get you down —make you feel tense, headachy, all worn out, just stop for a few minutes and take a "Bayer Break"! Thanks to instant flaking action, Bayer brings the fastest, gentlest relief you can get from hot-weather aches and pains. Next time you feel "heat beat," take a "Bayer Break." We promise you'll feel better fast!

BAYER ASPIRIN
FAST PAIN RELIEF

Actually, aspirin wasn't synthesized until 1893 when Felix Hoffmann, a chemist with Friedrich Bayer & Company of Germany, set out to find a remedy for his father's arthritis. Focusing the majority of his efforts on salicylate compounds, Felix hit upon something called acetylsalicylic acid, a pain reliever developed in 1853 by a Bavarian chemist named Charles Frederic von Gerhardt.

Von Gerhardt based much of his research on the fact that humankind had consistently turned toward the chemical attributes of a member of the Salicaceae family, a.k.a. the willow tree, for pain reduction. From ancient times to the Middle Ages to precolonial

America, willow leaves and roots were used for every medicinal purpose from earaches to gout.

Apparently, salicin, a white crystalline chemical housed in willows, is instrumental in reducing the production of hormonelike substances called prostaglandins. An excess of prostaglandins causes platelets to clot, whereby blood flows less freely, slowing transport of oxygen to the heart, brain, and other organs. Conversely, when prostaglandins are reduced, blood flows freely, and oxygen makes its way to one's organs in copious amounts.

Felix Hoffmann, with colleagues Arthur Eichengrun and Heinrich Dreser, developed, tested, and eventually found a commercial method by which to produce acetylsalicylic acid, or ASA. By 1898, they were doling out free samples to doctors throughout Germany.

What could they call their terrifically popular invention? How aspirin received its name is still not entirely clear, but rumor has it that the trio from Bayer started with "a" from "acetylsalicylic" and coupled it with the "spirea" of the spirea plant, which also yields salicin. *A-spirea*, of course, soon morphed into *aspirin*.

Bayer initially dispensed aspirin in powdered form, but in 1900 they introduced the drug in tablet form—an innovation that was welcomed by the public. Some years later, Sterling Drug acquired the Bayer Company, and they've been relieving aches and pains ever since. The Bayer product line has grown to include such specialized variations as Extra Strength Bayer Aspirin, Bayer Children's Chewable Aspirin, and Bayer PM.

Today, more than 20 tons of aspirin are sold every year, making aspirin the miracle drug of the 20th century.

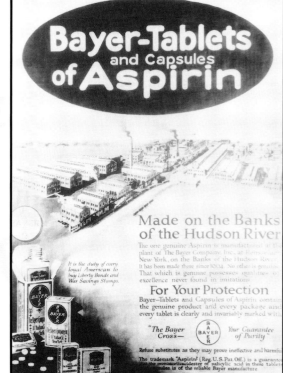

19

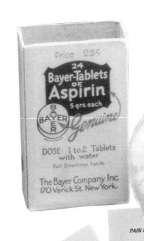

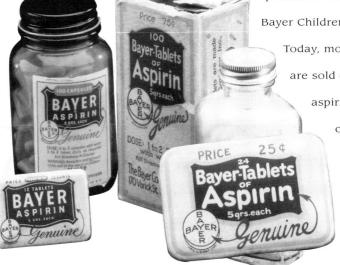

BUCK KNIVES

The legend of the Buck Knife is yet another tale in which necessity once again proves to be the mother of invention. The story begins in 1902. A 13-year-old apprentice blacksmith in Leavenworth, Kansas, by the name of Hoyt Heath Buck was charged with the daily chore of sharpening local farmers' hoes.

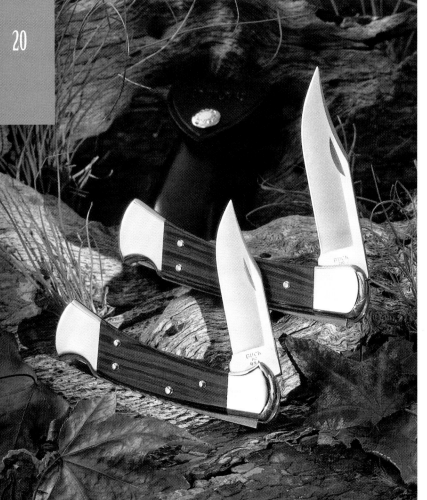

The tools so quickly lost their edge that, in his spare time, the resourceful Hoyt experimented with ways of making the edges stay sharp despite constantly scraping and slamming against hardened soil.

Tampering with various tempering processes, Hoyt eventually hit upon a method that won him considerable respect and admiration in his small Kansas town. After perfecting his craft, he applied it to many of the worn-out rasps lying about the shop. Suddenly, he found himself with a growing number of sharp-edged knives, none of which ever seemed to dull.

Having discovered such a unique heat-treating process, one would think that this young Buck would be well be on his way to fame and fortune. Not exactly. By age 18, he had gone west to Tacoma, Washington, and left his invention behind.

Cut to 1941. On the heels of Pearl Harbor, the U.S. government needed more knives for their fighting boys and turned to the American public. The call went out for citizens to donate their pocket knives to the war effort. Hoyt, by then 52 years old, was a pastor at the Assembly of God Church. He didn't own any knives and certainly hadn't made one in years, but he sure as heck knew how.

Setting up a little blacksmith shop in the church basement, he began handcrafting knives for servicemen. In no time at all, word of these Buck knives gained such popularity in the military community that GIs no longer in the service were writing in their orders. The problem was, Hoyt needed help.

In 1946, he and his wife, Daisy, packed up their belongings and headed to their son Alfred's house in San Diego. After much coaxing, Al joined the team, and H.H. Buck & Son opened their doors to the public. At first making only 25 knives a week, the company struggled terribly for nearly 20 years. But Al, assisted by his wife and his son, Chuck (now president of the company), persevered.

With a capital boost of $30,000 and the help of a man named Howard Craig, Buck Knives pulled themselves up from the cellar. And in 1964, the company designed and launched their world-famous Folding Hunter knife, firmly positioning them on the cutting edge of the knife-making industry. To date, the company has sold over 12 million Folding Hunters.

NEW POPULAR ALL-PURPOSE SIZE of BUCK

LIFETIME KNIFE
THAT CUTS ANYTHING

HAND MADE

EVEN CUTS BOLTS WITHOUT HARM TO BLADE

3½" HAND HOLLOW GROUND BLADE

7 INCHES OVER ALL

No. 108

$5 POSTPAID

This Buck Lifetime Knife is a genuine product of the Old West, used by Forest Rangers and skilled hunters. Outdoorsmen everywhere say there's no finer knife made ... no other that keeps its edge so long! The special high carbon steel blade is tempered by a Buck Family secret process to last a lifetime. The blade is hollow ground to razor sharpness ... yet it's so strong you can cut anything. Yes, easily cut a bolt in two without damaging the blade. A beauty for looks, too, with hand-carved lucite handle (black, red, green or blue) and a handmade saddle leather sheath. At your dealer's or clip this ad and mail with check or money order. No. 108 (shown above) is a new popular size. Other Buck Knives are: No. 113, Skinning Knife, 4-in. heavy blade, $9. No. 105, All-Purpose Knife, 5-in. blade, $7. No. 107, Fishing Knife, 3½-in. blade, $5.25. Both the 105 and 107 in one double sheath, $11. Satisfaction guaranteed. Prompt delivery. State knives and handle colors wanted.

THIS IS THE MAN WHO MAKES 'EM H.H. BUCK

BUCK LIFETIME KNIFE

H. H. BUCK and SON
1272 Morena Blvd., San Diego, California
Rush to me at once_____Buck Lifetime
Knives at $ each. Handle Color_____
Name_____
Address_____
City_____ Zone_____ State_____
(In California add 2½% State Sales Tax)   OL-10

OUTDOOR LIFE 1948

BURBERRYS OF LONDON

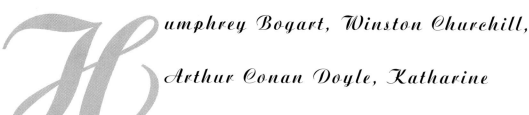

Humphrey Bogart, Winston Churchill, Arthur Conan Doyle, Katharine Hepburn, George Bernard Shaw, Marlene Dietrich, Rudyard Kipling. All of these legendary names wore a Burberrys coat.

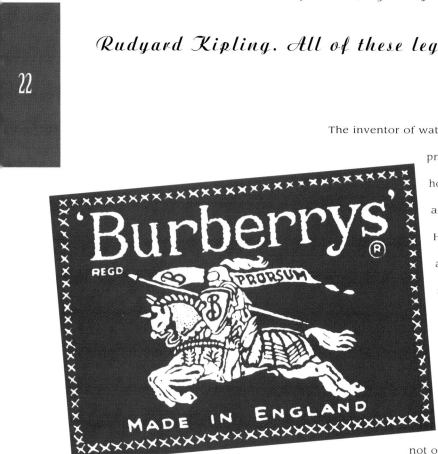

The inventor of waterproof clothing, Thomas Burberry began his rise to prominence as a young apprentice to a country draper in his hometown of Brockham-Greene in Surrey, England. In 1856, at the age of 21, Thomas journeyed to nearby Basingstoke, Hampshire, where he started his own venture. There he had a career-altering conversation with a local doctor on the shortcomings of the cumbersome mackintosh.

It was the doctor's opinion that it would be better to be soaked through than to be trapped inside a mackintosh, as the rubber lining provided no air ventilation. The wheels in Thomas' mind were set in motion.

Noticing that the linen smocks of local shepherds not only kept them dry but also remained comfortable in warm weather, Thomas took a closer look. He ascertained that the closely woven fabric sealed out moisture, yet allowed for ample ventilation.

After experimenting with a multitude of materials, Thomas found the secret to dressing for weather's fickle ways. He created a tightly woven cotton garment he called gabardine.

And how did he hit upon this term? He turned to the writings of his countryman, William Shakespeare. In *The Tempest*, Trinculo says, "I hid me under the dead moon calf's gaberdine for fear of the storm."

In 1899, Burberry coats, advertised as "suitable for India and the Colonies," had become so popular that the business relocated to London. Soon after, branches opened in New York, Paris, Buenos Aires, and Montevideo.

The company moved to their present location in London's Haymarket in 1912. There, Thomas Burberry experienced his greatest moment of triumph. Burberrys may have been all the rage among British officers, but the king's fighting men required the utmost protection to endure the rigors of World War I.

By weaving the fabric into the tightest possible gabardine, Burberry intensified its waterproofing feature. He then double-stitched all the seams and added storm flaps at the chest and on the pockets for greater protection. These special coats, he felt, would be suitable for England's finest while fighting in the trenches. A sort of "trench coat," if you will.

With ringing endorsements from King Edward VII, who was known to say "Get me my Burberry" whenever he need his favorite overcoat, to Captain Roald Amundsen, who led the first successful expedition to the South Pole, it's hard to imagine a time when Burberrys wasn't fully entrenched in our culture.

C O A T S

CALLAWAY

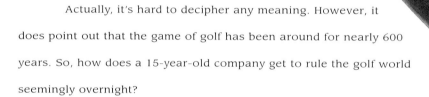

According to the <u>Oxford English Dictionary</u>, the first appearance of golf in any written form occurred in 1457 in the Scottish Acts Jas. 2 and reads: "And at ye fut bal ande ye golf be otterly cryt downe and nocht osyt."

Actually, it's hard to decipher any meaning. However, it does point out that the game of golf has been around for nearly 600 years. So, how does a 15-year-old company get to rule the golf world seemingly overnight?

In 1982, Ely Callaway purchased a fledgling company whose total sales brought in just under $365,000. At the time, Ely was 62, an age when most are winding down their careers. Not Mr. Callaway, whose long corporate path in the textile industry led to the purchase of a vineyard in the mid-1970s.

After what amounted to a few short years, Ely sold his vineyard in 1981 for a profitable $14 million and turned to his favorite pastime, the Sport of Kings.

Later that year, while golfing in Palm Springs, he came across a hickory-shafted wedge with a reinforced steel core. Ely was so impressed

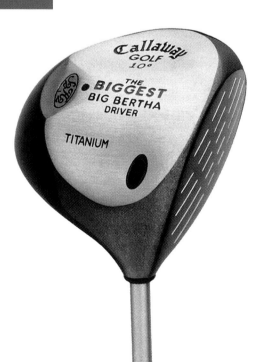

with its beauty and precision that he called the manufacturers to express his great appreciation. Oh, what a fateful call that proved to be!

What Ely learned was that the manufacturing company, run by three young men, was in dire financial straits and in need of a substantial stroke of good fortune. A few months later, Ely took 2.5 of his $14 million and gave his name to the company, providing the venture with a legitimate start time.

During its first five years, the company, then known as Callaway Hickory Stick, operated at a deficit. Establishing themselves slowly in the golf world, the four partners didn't enjoy a particularly promising life. It wasn't until 1988 that they were able to chip themselves out of the rough.

That year they changed their firm's name to Callaway Golf and introduced a new line of signature clubs that proved extremely profitable. Sales had jumped to an impressive $54 million, which, one might think, would be reason enough to sit back and enjoy the ride. Again, not Mr. Callaway.

Ely then introduced the legendary Big Bertha, named after a famed World War I cannon. This new line of drivers was such a sensation that by 1993, sales had soared to $255 million.

CAMPBELL'S

It's cold out. Really cold. You can barely feel your fingers after building the snowman that now stands guard on the front lawn. Your mom calls you in for lunch. You step into the kitchen. On the menu? A grilled cheese sandwich and Campbell's Tomato Soup. Ah, paradise!

Founded in 1869 as Anderson & Campbell, a cannery, Campbell's Soup Company in its first 28 years was, believe it or not, entirely soupless. Then, in 1897, long after Mr. Anderson had been bought out and six years after Mr. Campbell's retirement, the firm had become known as the Joseph Campbell Preserve Company. The reins of leadership had fallen into the trusty hands of a Mr. Arthur Dorrance.

That summer, Arthur's nephew, John T. Dorrance, returned from Germany after receiving his Ph.D. in organic chemistry. While preparing for a sail down the Delaware, John asked his uncle to stock the ship with Campbell's canned goods. But much to his chagrin, he learned that of their 200 product varieties, soup was not among them.

At the time, America's problem with manufacturing and selling ready-to-serve soup was that such an item was simply too bulky and expensive to ship. But John had an idea, based on the fact that the amount of water that went into preparing soup was

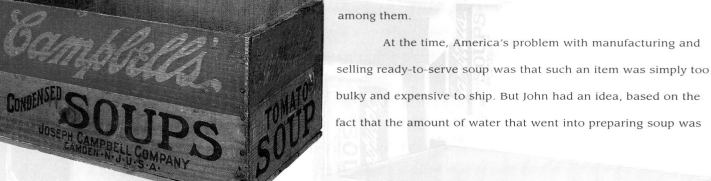

responsible for the majority of the weight and, therefore, the shipping cost.

Putting his organic chemistry training to use, he cut the amount of water in half and experimented with condensed liquids that were saucelike in consistency. The idea was to let "housewives" add the water to the product themselves. Dr. Dorrance's innovation resulted in the first five Campbell's soups to be shipped: Tomato, Consommé, Vegetable, Chicken, and the much-beloved Oxtail.

Manufacturing at the rate of 10 cases a week, Campbell's showed a $60,000 loss by the end of the 1897 fiscal year. Dr. Dorrance determined then to take it to the streets. After extensive cooking demonstrations and ad campaigns, Campbell's soon became a staple in family cupboards. By 1905, those 10 cases had grown to 40,000 a week, and Campbell's had racked up an impressive $900,000 in sales—$750,000 of which were attributed to soup.

Now in its 128th year, with a history of quality and ever-growing global recognition (some of which is due to Andy Warhol), Campbell's Soup is sold in over 120 countries and the company's overall sales have topped the $6 billion mark. In addition to their ever-popular condensed soups, which includes top sellers Cream of Mushroom, Chicken Noodle, and Tomato, the company has added lines such as Healthy Request, Chunky, Home Cookin', and Ramen. And world travelers can find soups created in response to cultural differences, like Watercress & Duck Gizzard in China, or Cream of Chili Poblano in Mexico. Mmmm, mmmm, good!

S O U P

CHANEL NO. 5

Chanelegance. The words seem to blend effortlessly into one another, befitting the Executrix of Élan, Gabrielle "Coco" Chanel, a woman whose very name is synonymous with style. She redefined, if not invented, fashion for the 20th century.

Having received her seamstress' training during a two-year stay at a convent, Coco—who derived her sobriquet as a chanteuse when she inquired "Qui qu'a vu Coco?"—first supported herself in the late 1800s as a milliner in a Moulins boutique.

After several years performing on stage, she secured enough connections to pursue a life among the Parisian aristocracy. Her first venture into couture was as a designer and manufacturer of women's hats. Her clientele, personality, and innovations eventually won her great popularity and, by as early as 1910, Chanel Modes were the toast of the town.

Then, in 1921, Grand Duke Dmitri Pavlovitch, grandson of Czar Alexander II and Coco's current love interest, introduced her to a Parisian chemist named Ernest Beaux. Perfumes at the time were extremely heady and obtrusive, and Chanel was interested in creating a fragrance that epitomized her refined, streamlined style.

After combining over 80 ingredients, the jasmine-based essence was complete. Chanel designed the "pharmaceutical" bottle herself and selected the name No. 5 simply because it was her favorite number. But, being an extremely shrewd businesswoman, Coco realized that it would be unwise for her to launch the product on a wide scale. Having no past experience in the perfume industry, she was determined to build slowly, à la her success as a couturière.

Early in her career, Coco was a proponent of the idea that if one wanted a luxury item to sell, one needed the rich and famous to think they were responsible for the product's success. Armed with this ideology, she atomized the fitting rooms in her salons until her clientele began asking for the fragrance. Coco coyly replied that she had only enough bottles to send out as gifts, but if they considered the fragrance marketable, she'd sell it.

And did she ever! Chanel No. 5, the first perfume ever to bear a couturier's name, was so immediately successful that after two years, Coco found herself unhappily distracted from her real love, designing clothing.

In 1923, she made the acquaintance of Paul and Pierre Wertheimer, the owners of Les Parfumeries Bourjois, France's largest cosmetic and fragrance company. The two men agreed to take on all aspects of Chanel No. 5, manufacturing and marketing in exchange for 90 percent of the profits. Coco's mere 10 percent nevertheless enabled her to live out her remaining 48 years in a style befitting the First Lady of Fashion.

She seems to have left her creation in good hands. With prices ranging from $88 for the $1/4$-ounce bottle to $245 for the largest one, Bloomingdale's reports that Chanel No. 5 is still selling strong.

SODA POP
COCA-COLA

Recognized as the most successful product in the history of commerce, Coca-Cola is sold in more than 200 countries, amounting to hundreds of millions of servings a day. Not too shabby for a product that was invented in the backyard of a pharmacist's home.

30

On May 8, 1886, Dr. John Styth Pemberton produced the syrup for Coca-Cola in a three-legged brass pot at his Atlanta, Georgia, home. He then poured his new elixir into a jug, lugged it down to Jacob's Pharmacy, and began selling it for five cents a pop. True, this was a little pricey in those days, but the early reviews were nothing short of raves. "Excellent, delicious, refreshing," cried those on the scene. Little did they know that they were tasting the stuff of legend.

Soon after, carbonated water was added to the syrup. It's not known whether Dr. Pemberton had intended Coca-Cola to be consumed as such, but suffice it to say, the marriage between the two

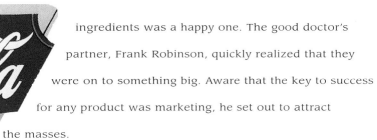

ingredients was a happy one. The good doctor's partner, Frank Robinson, quickly realized that they were on to something big. Aware that the key to success for any product was marketing, he set out to attract the masses.

First on Frank's agenda was to create an eye-catching sign worthy of a revolutionary fountain drink. After experimenting with a few styles, Frank settled on the now-famous script still in use today. He hung a banner outside Jacob's Pharmacy, but even this wasn't enough. After all, what was Coca-Cola? Dr. Pemberton and Frank then had a brainstorm: add the word *drink*. The craze for cola soon began.

In 1888, just a few short years after his invention, Dr. Pemberton sold off the majority of his business to Asa G. Candler, an Atlanta businessman. Three years later, Candler bought out his co-investors for the sizable sum of $2,300 and got down to business.

Candler opened syrup-manufacturing plants, and in 1899, he granted the exclusive bottling rights to three Tennesseeans, who formed what is known today as the worldwide Coca-Cola bottling system. In 1916, the Root Glass Company of Terre Haute, Indiana, replaced the beverage's straight-sided bottle with the contoured design that has become perhaps the most recognized symbol throughout the world.

The Candler era ended in 1919, when Ernest Woodruff and friends purchased Coca-Cola for a paltry $25 million. Woodruff's son, Robert, then began his six-decade reign. His vision and leadership are largely responsible for the phenomenon that "Coke" (coined in 1945) has since become.

COLEMAN LAMPS

Born in 1870, William C. Coleman had been teaching for several years in the Kansas school system when he came upon a brilliant gadget called the Efficient Lamp. A self-proclaimed amateur salesman, W.C. was so taken with the gasoline-burning lamp that he just had to contact the manufacturers.

It turned out that the owner of the item was the Irby-Gilliland Company of Memphis, Tennessee. Coleman was convinced that this innovation, coupled with his salesman's acumen, would bring light to the masses. So, on January 1, 1900, Coleman hit the road.

His first stop was the town of Kingfisher in the Oklahoma Territory. Coleman was sure that he'd be contacting the Irby-Gilliland Company for a new shipment almost immediately, but after a tireless week, the Efficient Lamp sold a scant two units.

Coleman explained to the good people of Kingfisher that his lamp was different from the rest. Not only did it burn gasoline, but when air was pumped into the lantern's reservoir, a valve opened, allowing the air pressure to force the gas into a generator. The generator was then heated with an alcohol torch that vaporized the fuel. The released vapor, once mingled with air, ignited with an intense brightness. There was really nothing to it.

LANTERNS

Still, there were no takers, and when Coleman inquired as to why, he learned that a salesman had come through earlier with an inferior brand of lantern and hustled many of Kingfisher's citizens. Ever astute, Coleman pursued a different tack.

Rather than sell lamps, W.C. set about selling light. He rented the Efficient Lamps for $1 a week and threw in fuel and service at no extra charge. If customers saw no light, Coleman assured them he'd see no money. And with that, by the end of January 1900, the Coleman Company was under way.

After two solid years, Coleman moved his operation to Wichita, Kansas, and by that time had earned enough money to purchase all the rights to the Efficient Lamp. He changed the name to the Arc Lamp and proudly stamped "Made in Wichita, Kansas U.S.A." across the front. By 1905, he embarked on manufacturing his very own brand of gas-burning lamps, and Coleman's future shined more brightly than ever.

Although the Coleman line has grown to include stoves and other camping equipment, the lantern remains the company's hallmark. At last tally, over 50 million lanterns have been sold.

CONVERSE ALL STAR

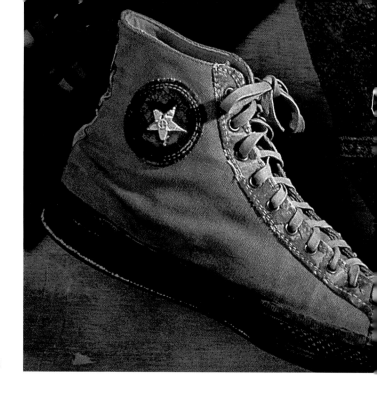

It was 1892, and Dr. James Naismith of Springfield, Massachusetts, was gaining notoriety for the simple act of having hung a peach basket from a gymnasium wall. Perhaps this doesn't seem too significant, but what Dr. Naismith actually did was invent the game of basketball.

The early 20th century witnessed great enthusiasm over this burgeoning pastime. Known as a journeyman with a jumpshot, Charles H. "Chuck" Taylor, a player for both the Buffalo Germans and the Akron Firestones, was one of the country's first great cagers.

At about the same time that Chuck began takin' it to the hoop, Marquis M. Converse was trying to figure out what to do with some venture capital. Having a penchant for the rubber trade, Marquis started up an operation called the Converse Rubber Company in 1908.

Basing his firm in Malden, Massachusetts, just 90 miles east of the birthplace of basketball, Converse hired a small crew of 15, and in 1909, they produced their very first line of shoes.

Initial sales went through the roof, and less than a year later, this fledgling operation grew to a workforce of 360 men and women producing over 4,000 shoes per day. Converse was clearly on to something, but it would be another seven years before they'd slam-dunk the competition.

In 1917, cashing in on the basketball mania sweeping the nation, Marquis produced the famed Converse All Star, a canvas, rubber-soled sneaker that came up high on the ankle for lateral movement and support. And Chuck Taylor fell in love with them. He latched on to a pair of these high-tops, and before you could say "pick and roll," Converse All Star sneakers were gracing the feet of some of "round ball's" finest.

By 1921, Chuck hung up his high-tops and signed on as a traveling salesman with the Converse Company. Setting up clinics around the country, he so popularized the shoe that his signature was added to the famed ankle patch in 1923. His efforts also earned him the epithet "Ambassador to Basketball." Today, thanks to Chuck, Converse has sold nearly 550 million pairs of that very same shoe. Take that, Shaq!

FABER-CASTELL

Lothar von Faber, fourth in line to the A.W. Faber dynasty, set out in 1839 with the following mission statement: "To make the best of what is made in the world." Up until that time, the Faber family had been making a modest living in the pencil trade. Caspar Faber, Lothar's great-grandfather and founder of the dynasty, is not, however, credited with the invention of the pencil. The writing implement had been around in crude form since the mid-1500s.

It is thought that the first pencils hailed from England and later came into widespread use when chemist Karl Willhelm unearthed a particular form of carbon in the mines of the Cumberland Mountains. He named his discovery graphite.

England immediately went into a pencil frenzy and, with the mines nearly depleted in just a few short years, an export ban was placed on this "black gold." In fact, any violation of the ban was punishable by death.

FABER-CASTELL
since 1761

This, of course, upended the Faber family business. By the turn of the 19th century, pencils became little more than ornate wood casings with scarcely any graphite filling. And, to make matters worse, they cost a fortune. But brighter times were on the horizon.

After Lothar assumed control of the operation in 1839, he adopted a process that involved combining graphite and clay to produce pencils with varying degrees of hardness; this compensated for the dearth of "black gold."

Soon Lothar von Faber's newfound success allowed him to purchase a graphite mine in Siberia in 1856. With the depletion of England's resources, this enabled Faber to establish such a stronghold that he was awarded a knighthood six years later.

Later strokes of brilliance included the six-sided pencil design, eventually pilfered by all manufacturers. He was also the first to etch his name onto a writing instrument, thereby making Faber indistinguishable from pencil.

How did Castell cash in on the company craft? In 1898, Lothar's granddaughter married Count Alexander zu Castell-Ruedenhausen. Seven years later, Faber-Castell made its first appearance when the count designed the classic green Castell 9000.

FILOFAX

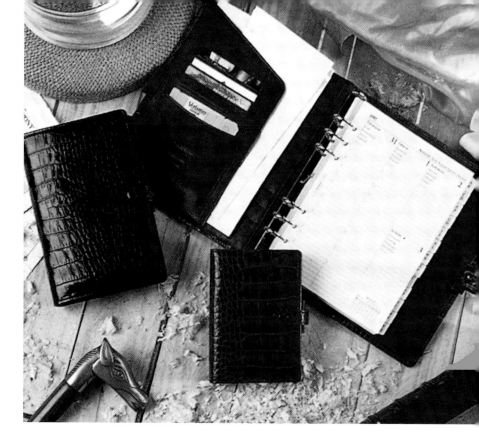

At the end of World War I, a British Army officer by the name of Colonel Disney was due to return to his native England when he came across a curious leather folder. This loose-leafed entity contained materials varying from engineering to scientific to technical documents. Little did Colonel Disney know that he was, in fact, holding the world's very first Filofax.

Such an extraordinarily brilliant concept demanded further investigation, thought Disney, who immediately contacted his mates back in the motherland. If marketed properly, this personal organizer could become extremely popular among professionals. The following year, Disney arrived home and set about the business of securing the necessary manufacturing and distribution

rights throughout the United Kingdom. With a small office space, a box of samples, and a temporary secretary by the name of Grace Scurr, Disney commenced his operation under the name Norman and Hill Ltd.

Interestingly, it was his secretary, Ms. Scurr, who kept referring to Colonel Disney's brainchild as a "file of facts." So taken was she with the product that she continued in her "temporary" job for more than 30 years.

Legend holds that one of the many reasons Ms. Scurr was such a proponent of her employer's invention involved the blitzkrieg bombing of London. While on her way to work the following morning, she was stopped by an air raid warden who informed her that the Norman and Hill offices had been obliterated.

Fortunately, all of the company's customer records were safe within the pages of Ms. Scurr's very own Filofax and, because of her resourcefulness (and foresight), documents vital to the functioning of the business survived. Ms. Scurr was later rewarded when she became chairperson of Norman and Hill, a position she held until her retirement in the late 1950s.

GIBSON

Gibson 1894 100 YEARS 1994

40

*I*t's hard to talk about Orville Gibson and the impact he had on the world of music without providing a list of the 20th century's all-time great guitarists, all of whom scaled tremendous heights thanks to their Gibson guitars. So, in no particular order:

Robert Johnson, Les Paul, Chuck Berry, B.B. King, Eric Clapton, Jimi Hendrix, Keith Richards, Neil Young, Charlie Daniels, Travis Tritt, ZZ Top's Billy Gibbons, Chet Atkins, Robert Cray, George Thorogood, U2's The Edge, Frank Zappa, Pete Townshend, Jimmy Buffett, jazz great Joe Pass, the legendary Django Reinhardt, Duane Allman, the Doors' Robby Krieger, the Everly Brothers, Jeff Beck, blues great John Lee Hooker, Led Zeppelin's Jimmy Page, T-Bone Walker, Bill Haley, and Guns N' Roses' Slash; even Diana Ross strummed a Gibson B-25, although none of her picking ever made any recording session.

The list reads like a page out of Who's Who in the Rock and Roll Hall of Fame. But just who was this Leonardo da Vinci of stringed instrument design who set the world of music on such an irreversible course?

GUITARS

Born in upstate New York in 1856, Orville Gibson hung around the Empire State for 25 years before he packed his bags and headed west for Kalamazoo, Michigan. It's not known why he chose this locale. After all, it wasn't the home of any particular style of music, nor was it a town in the throes of expansion. All 25-year-old Orville knew was that time was on his side and he had a certain dance with destiny.

After 13 years of working various jobs, he experimented with instrument design, creating an innovative method for fashioning new mandolins. He filed his first patent for an instrument that looked somewhat like a violin on steroids. According to Walter Carter, author of *Gibson Guitars: 100 Years of an American Icon*, Orville created a mandolin with a "violin-style carved soundboard and backboard." This design he would later apply toward guitars as well.

Soon Gibson had gained renown for his artistry and was approached to set up a limited partnership. Accepting a $2,500 offer for the manufacture and design of "guitars, mandolins, mandolas, lutes, and other stringed instruments," he began the Gibson Mandolin-Guitar Mfg. Co., Ltd., in 1902.

Orville didn't stay with the company for very long and returned to his family's home in 1909. He was in poor health and, sadly, passed away less than a decade later, never seeing his brilliance come to such widespread fruition. The company, armed with Orville's innovative designs, went on to fulfill his ambition and secure Gibson's place in music history.

41

HARIBO

Did you know that in Germany alone, the amount of Haribo Gummi Bears eaten can circle the world three times?

It all started in 1920 with Hans and Gertrude Riegel and a company called Heinen & Riegel. Nestled in Kessenich, near Bonn, Heinen & Riegel began with just eight employees.

What are Haribo bears made of? Well, basically, glucose syrup (that's what renders them translucent), sugar, dextrose (for sweetening), and, finally, gelatine (the ingredient that makes them gummy). These are supplemented with color extracts from plants and fruits, aromatic flavors, oil, and lemon. The exact recipe is a secret we're not allowed to tell.

Becoming a BearHaribo is an arduous task. First, the mixture is shot through a huge, dinosaurlike pipe. Then, the previously prepared flavored essences

and natural colors are added. On the assembly line, plaster Gold Bears are pressed into cornstarch, leaving behind their celebrated imprints. In mere seconds, jets inject the mixture via nozzles into the imprint. And that's how Gold Bears are born, 504 at a time—84 each of bright red, ruby red, yellow, white, green, and orange.

The bears are transported in boxes while still warm and fluid. Three or four days are allotted for them to dry. Afterward, a beeswax treatment glosses them up and prevents them from sticking to one other.

The classic Gold BearHaribo come in a variety of sizes. In addition to the "normal" size bear of 2.2 cm (that's nearly .9 inches), there are the 1.7 cm Mini Bears and the 11 cm Super Goldbears. In 1930, the company's slogan was "Haribo makes children happy." It took them only 30 years to add "and grownups as well." Proof for this claim? German talk-show host Thomas Gottschalk chews on them incessantly. Ex–foreign minister Hans Dietrich Genscher also has a weakness for them. He even travels with his BearHaribo.

Seventy million bears leave the production facilities in Europe every day. With numbers like that, there's no chance these bears will wind up on the endangered species list.

43

HARLEY-DAVIDSON

ou hear the name *Harley-Davidson*, and immediately the *Hell's Angels* come to mind: long-haired, heavily tattooed biker bad boys riding through the American heartland in the guise of modern-day desperadoes. Well, think again. Today's typical Harley owner is college educated and earns nearly $70,000 a year.

The history of the company reads like something out of the OK Corral, complete with Doc Holliday and the Earp brothers. What those gentlemen did for Wild West law and order, William Harley and the Davidson boys did for "Easy Riding" transportation.

It was in 1901 Milwaukee where Harley joined forces with Walter, William, and Arthur Davidson to create the first motor-assisted bicycle. This partnership initially had nothing to do with motorcycles at all, but rather was formed to build an outboard motor enabling anglers to beat rivals at the best fishing holes.

Intrigued by the powerful engine they had created, the boys enlisted the design assistance of Emil Kröger and set their sights on the open road. By 1903, the first Harley was introduced and the precursor to the Moped born.

In fact, this premier Harley was so similar to the Moped in design, it even had pedals. This was fortunate, considering that the single-cylinder two-horsepower engine wasn't nearly strong enough to carry a rider uphill. However, the bike design was revolutionary enough to urge Harley-Davidson on to bolder innovations.

It took a mere six years before they introduced their first two-cylinder, V-twin engine, producing that unmistakable rumbling destined to become the signature of Harley-Davidsons from then on. Shortly thereafter, the company found themselves with over 150 competitors in the motor-assisted bicycle business. Nevertheless, they struggled to keep up with orders.

World War I created an even greater demand for motorcycles overseas, but while other manufacturers focused on function, Harley added form to the mix. They were the first to stylize their gas tanks with the now-famous "teardrop" design. And, in the 1930s, they cashed in on the Art Deco craze by adding three-tone paints and decals.

Today, Harley-Davidson is the last remaining U.S. motorcycle manufacturer as well as the preferred choice of bike enthusiasts around the world. Just ask Arnold Schwarzenegger, Sylvester Stallone, Cher or Dwight Yoakam—they won't hesitate to tell you their choice for the true American classic.

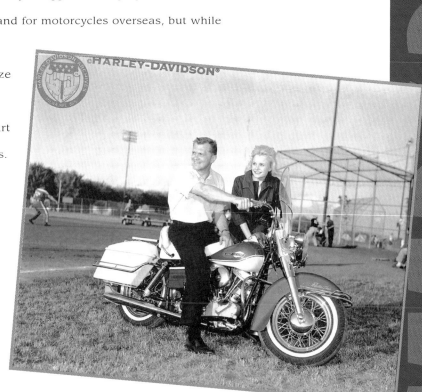

HARRY WINSTON

*B*egin with the luxury that is *Yves Saint Laurent. Stir in a dash of Chanel refinement. Then gently blend with the style of Fred Astaire. Simmer over a warm flame burning with the desire in millions of women's hearts and savor only the slightest taste of what it is to be Harry Winston.*

To enter the rarefied halls of Harry Winston's Rodeo Drive salon is to glide into the essence of every woman's fantasy—the world's foremost jewelry atelier.

The son of a New York jeweler, Harry showed a keen eye for his craft before he reached his teens. Once, while passing a store window display of "throwaway" rings, Harry spotted what must surely have been an emerald. He bought the ring for 25 cents, then turned around and sold it for a handsome profit. Little did he know that this simple act would lead to his handling over 60 of the world's 303 major diamonds, more than any other individual, including government heads and royalty. From the legendary Hope Diamond to the 94.80-carat Star of the East (recently sold for over $10 million) to the Lal Qila 72.76-carat green diamond sold to King Farouk of Egypt to the 69.42-carat Taylor-Burton diamond, Harry Winston has handled them all.

In 1932, at the age of 19, Harry began his company with very little money, very grand visions, and an ingenuity in design that would forever transform and revolutionize our jewel-bedazzled world. He tirelessly attended estate sale after estate sale, purchasing dozens of gems, only to recut, reset and resell them to an elite clientele whose names he culled from the pages of social registries.

One evening, while attending a Christmas party, Harry's attention was caught by the design of a yuletide wreath. He was struck by the notion that the leaves shaped the wreath. This, of course, led to his experimentation with lighter metals that allowed the precious stones themselves to shape the jewelry. The industry has never been the same since.

There have been many anecdotes about Harry Winston. When the friend of a certain Hollywood producer expressed surprise that patrons could actually be served lunch while shopping for the perfect diamond at Harry Winston's, the producer responded, "Honey, when you got a million bucks to spend on a diamond, the least they can do is bring you a sandwich."

And who can forget Marilyn Monroe's legendary line from her classic song, "Diamonds Are a Girl's Best Friend"? "Talk to me, Harry Winston," she sang. "Tell me all about it."

HEINZ KETCHUP

Ketchup fun fact number 351: Americans were not the first to discover ketchup. Rather, it's the Chinese who lay claim to originating the king of all condiments. Initially known as *ke-tsiap*, a tasty little pickled fish brine that was all the rage in Asia, "ketchup" didn't make its way westward until the late 1600s.

After a brief stint in Great Britain, where many a seamen aspired to simulate the savory stuff, a shortage of ingredients from the East resulted in a popular variation. Using walnuts, mushrooms, and cucumbers, ketchup soon found its way into the hearts, minds, and cupboards of some of England's elite. Why, even Lord Byron celebrated its virtue in his poem "Beppo."

So, bearing in mind its long, illustrious history, how on earth did ketchup become synonymous with

Heinz? And why, to this very day, do we sing the praises of Henry Heinz? For the simple fact that in 1876, Henry developed his timeless "catsup" recipe and became the first to mass market this much-coveted condiment.

It was fortunate for Henry that he didn't embark on making his mark until the late 1800s. A quarter century earlier, a significant breakthrough came in the form of a new ingredient...the tomato. Funny how we naturally connect tomatoes with ketchup, but in 1876, to do so was cutting edge.

Henry's blend owes a great deal to the exploits of Maine seafarers who, in the mid-1800s, coupled their penchant for pickled fish brine with the succulent tomatoes of Mexico and the West Indies. This new concoction gained rapid popularity throughout American households.

The problem was that it was extremely difficult to prepare. And not only that, but unpleasant (and unappetizing) aromas permeated American homes in the process. Why not be the first to produce a quality "catsup" and offer "blessed relief for Mother and the other women of the household"?

Soon the satisfying taste of Heinz Ketchup became the favorite of housewives who relished the idea of never having to go through the tedious (and noisome) process of preparation again.

Today, Heinz U.S.A. sells more than one billion 14-ounce bottles each year, which, if you do the math, works out to more than four bottles per American per year.

KETCHUP

HERMÉS KELLY BAG

The House of Hermés, founded in 1837 by Thierry Hermés, began as purveyors of fine harnesses, saddles, and other equestrian-related accessories. Targeting the Parisian aristocracy, Thierry quickly gained a reputation for unsurpassable artistry.

As the years passed and the need for tack was diminished by the advent of rail and automotive travel, the Hermés family knew they had to evolve with the times. Luggage, trunks, gloves, scarves, and handbags became the focus and quickly brought the family name to even greater prominence.

By the mid-1900s, Thierry's grandson, Emile-Maurice, had carried on the family tradition with great success. But then, a specific moment in history catapulted the House of Hermés through the stratosphere.

It was 1956, and a very pregnant Grace Kelly appeared on the cover of *Life* magazine. Reluctant to share her swollen belly with the world, Grace hid behind her oversized Hermés saddle bag, an Hautes à Courroises. This became such a celebrated image that women throughout the world were desperate to possess the same gorgeous accessory.

Originally designed as a saddle carrier for hunters in the mid-1800s, the bag was soon seen toted along the Champs-Elysées, Fifth Avenue, and Rodeo Drive—cleverly renamed the Kelly Bag, after Princess Grace.

Today, the Hermés reputation in the "quality-of-life business" remains unsullied. So committed to their workmanship is Hermés that bags are individually crafted; upon completion, each is numbered and signed. In fact, the process is so time-consuming that the waiting list for the $10,000 handbags extends up to a year.

B A G S

HOHNER HARMONICAS

Sixteen-year-old German inventor Christian Friedrich Buschmann dubbed his proto-harmonica the aura. An astute young entrepreneur, Christian registered the first European patents for his design right then and there in 1821 but was unable to develop the concept any further.

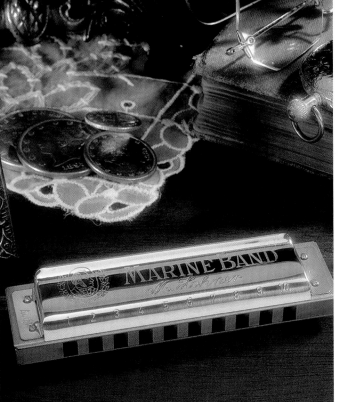

The new musical gadget quickly gained popularity but didn't enjoy its first major breakthrough until 1826, when an instrument maker named Richter created "a variation that consisted of 10 holes and 20 reeds, with separate blow and draw reed plates mounted on either side of a cedar comb."

This new design, known as the Mundharmonika, or mouth organ, incorporated a diatonic scale and set the standard by which all others would follow—or so Herr Richter would have us believe. But soon came the clock-maker Matthias Hohner.

In 1857, Hohner, employing his entire family and one craftsman, switched gears (so to speak) and manufactured 650 harmonicas for the German marketplace. The results were music to his ears.

Encouraged by the response, Hohner soon developed mass production capabilities and provided the device's ordinary appearance with a well-deserved makeover. Each Hohner harmonica was to bear the craftsman's name in a stylish, baroque cover plate.

In 1862, Hohner crossed the Atlantic and introduced his creation to the New World. The populace went wild. A mere 25 years later, the company began producing more than one million harmonicas a year. And, because Matthias was a shrewd businessman, he tapped the potential for increased sales through celebrity endorsements.

The Hohner #1896, which hit the music market in 1896 and has remained virtually unchanged to this day, was to become the world's most famous harmonica. With a ringing endorsement from famed bandmaster John Philip Sousa, whose own Marine Band lent its name to the instrument, the Hohner "Marine Band" Harmonica quickly swept the nation.

By the time of the Great Depression, an estimated 2,000 local "marine bands" had formed around the country. Even Irving Berlin, perhaps one of America's greatest songwriters, claimed that the first musical instrument he ever picked up was none other than a Hohner harmonica.

HONEY BEARS

O ne night in 1957, Ralph and Luella Gamber were having a quiet dinner in their Lancaster, Pennsylvania, home with fellow beekeepers, Woodrow and Rita Miller, from California. The conversation turned to honey, as it usually did, and the evening's topic was finding a convenient method to dispense their very sticky, but delicious, product.

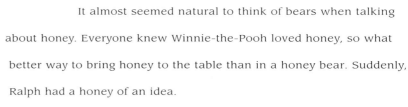

It almost seemed natural to think of bears when talking about honey. Everyone knew Winnie-the-Pooh loved honey, so what better way to bring honey to the table than in a honey bear. Suddenly, Ralph had a honey of an idea.

Eleven years earlier, he purchased three hives of bees at a farm sale for $27. Beekeeping became Ralph's hobby when he was not out on the road as a salesman for the Armour Meat Company. Luella began packing honey in her kitchen for Ralph to peddle on the side. Well, thought Ralph,

bears loves honey; why not create a honey dispenser that looks like one.

After some investigating, Ralph found the Olympics Plastic Company in California. They were willing to work with him in his quest to bring the honey bear to reality. After several prototypes, Ralph was satisfied with the design and the first honey bear molds were made. What was unique about this bear was his toes!

Ralph had spoken with an attorney about getting a patent on his new container, but was told even the slightest change in the honey bear's design would invalidate the patent. Thus to keep the original bear unique, it had six toes! Yes the bear was adorable, with its chubby belly and affectionate smile, but what would the consumers think?

The following year, Yogi Bear made his television debut—and sales were given a sweet boost.

The initial payment of $27 in 1946 for those three beehives had a remarkable return on investment. Now in 1997, 85-year-old Ralph Gamber is the proud papa of a company that sells 2.7 million cuddly, six-toed bears and packs over 40 million pounds of honey each year.

HONEY

HUSH PUPPIES

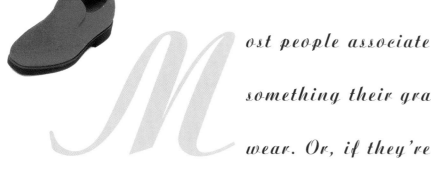

*M*ost people associate Hush Puppies with something their grandfather might wear. Or, if they're from the South, it's some kind of fried cornmeal edible. But one glance at the new Hush Puppy catalog, packed with supermodel hipsters photographed by Richard Avedon, and Hush Puppies are due for another look!

Created in 1958 by Victor Krause, CEO of the U.S. footwear company Wolverine World Wide, Inc., Hush Puppies came into being circuitously via a major world conflict, owing its existence in part to the Korean War.

In the early fifties, Wolverine was called upon to create a certain style of footwear that involved tanning pigskin for GIs to wear comfortably below the 38th parallel. Following the war, Krause resolved not to let this new technology slip through his fingers and quickly set himself to work.

After several years of experimentation, Wolverine came forth with an innovative category of shoe, "Casual Footwear." They put their first foot forward with a classic suede oxford shoe on a thick crepe sole. This new line was affordable and far more comfortable than the wingtip shoes of the time. Yet, interestingly, these

S H O E S

shoes weren't called Hush Puppies at all.

Not long after their introduction, a Wolverine salesman by the name of Jim Muir was traveling down in Tennessee when he stopped to have dinner with an old friend. During the course of the meal, Jim's pal was so tired of his hounds barking that he began to toss them hush puppies, the aforementioned fried cornmeal balls.

The dogs were instantly assuaged, but Jim's mind started racing. The food was called hush puppies, and feet were called dogs. In fact, aching feet were commonly referred to as barking dogs. Well, the hush puppies quieted down his friend's dogs just like the Wolverine shoes soothed one's aching feet, so a legend was born.

Since then, Hush Puppies have taken the world by storm. They are also bridging the age gap like never before. No, not because Tom Hanks wore them in the closing scene of *Forrest Gump*, but rather because of the casualness of today's trendy Generation X. Just ask designer Anna Sui or *GQ* fashion editor Bruce Pask or folks at the Gap—if you're not wearing Hush Puppies, let's face it, you're sleeping with the dogs.

Saddle slip-on in Silver Dollar (shown). Wild Oats, Black, Yucca Tan, Corn Cob. Men's sizes only—6 to 12. Narrow, medium widths only.

Sport oxford in Wild Oats (shown), White, Silver Dollar, Houn' Dawg, Yucca Tan, Scarlet Feather, Caviar. Men's sizes only—6 to 12.

57

Men's raglan oxford in Tumbleweed (shown), Wild Oats, Caviar, Corn Cob, White. Sizes 6 to 12. Boys' in Tumbleweed, Wild Oats, Caviar. Sizes 2 to 6.

INTERNATIONAL WATCH COMPANY

A *t $275,000—not exactly in the category of impulse purchases—J.W.C. watches enjoy the reputation of possessing perhaps the finest, most precise mechanism in the world of horology.*

Setting his sights on Europe in 1868, 27-year-old Bostonian and company co-founder Florentine A. Jones arrived in Switzerland. A young idealist with an engineering background, Jones wanted to commingle his automatization expertise with that of world-renowned Swiss precision.

Upon his arrival, he was surprised to find that timepiece manufacture was literally a cottage industry. Jones set about proposing his concepts to various craftspeople and was stunned when they responded with a vague neutrality. The basic problem was that the Swiss were concerned that modernization of the industry would eventually render them superfluous.

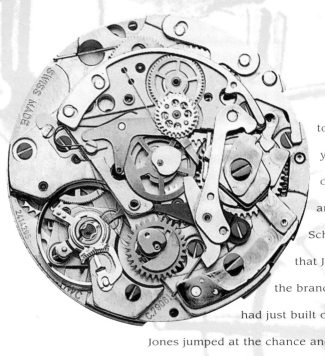

Jones nevertheless stuck to his grand vision, and later that year, he made the acquaintance of Johann Heinrich Moser, an industrialist from Schaffhausen. Moser suggested that Jones move his equipment into the brand-new hydroelectric plant Moser had just built on the banks of the Rhine. Jones jumped at the chance and installed his equipment, the majority of which came from America. The two men began their operation immediately, and in no time, Jones had produced his very first "movement," the Jones Calibre. This pocket watch was so far ahead of its time that, although not produced much past the 1880s, many of its parts are still on hand and can be ordered through I.W.C.

In 1880, Jones and Moser were bought out by machine manufacturer and fellow Schaffhausenite Johannes Rauschenbach-Vogel. Johannes took over I.W.C. and began a four-generation dynastic run that boasted the creation of such legendary watches as the Mark XI, the Mark XII, and the Il Destriero Scafusia, known as the world's most complex watch. In fact, the catalog suggests a direct call for a price quote.

Over the years, I.W.C. designs have found themselves on the wrists and in the pockets of many of the world's most prominent figures: from popes to tsars to politicians to explorers. Notably, Sir Edmund Hillary wore an I.W.C. Ingenieur while conquering Mount Everest.

WATCHES

IVORY SOAP

There is but one product in the United States whose very mention reaffirms all that is right with this country, whose name is synonymous with purity, goodness, and family values. That product is Ivory Soap, single-handedly responsible for cleaning up America since 1879.

William Procter and James Gamble, whose company would become the proud makers of Ivory, first joined forces in 1837. Candle-maker William had left London after his shop burned down, and soap-stylist James had fled the Irish famine of 1819. They soon found themselves settled in Cincinnati, Ohio, each married to the daughters of Alexander Norris.

Father-in-law Norris played a significant role in the development of Procter & Gamble for it was he who commented on the fact that the trades of both used lye, grease, tallow, and other oils in their base. Why not pair up, suggested Alexander? So pair up they did.

Business picked up during the Civil War when they supplied soap to the Union Army in the west. Flying high from this boom, P&G started working to develop new technologies in cake soap production.

Under the leadership of Gamble's son, James N. Gamble, Procter & Gamble introduced its white soap in 1879. Whence the name Ivory? Drawing inspiration from the Scriptures, William's son, Harley, had read in Psalm 45: "All thy garments smell of myrrh, and aloes, and cassia, out of the ivory palaces whereby they have made thee glad."

It's not known why Harley focused on the word *ivory* in this passage, but whatever the reason, not only did he convince the company's board to accept the name, but, shockingly, he also suggested they advertise as well. Back in 1882, advertising was associated with disreputable companies that used the practice to peddle inferior wares. Most of these companies would falsely state that their products were "100 percent" effective. Wanting to distance themselves from such misleading claims, Procter & Gamble introduced Ivory Soap as being "99 $\frac{44}{100}$ percent pure." As one might surmise, the campaign was successful...to say the least.

Soon, Ivory Soap was scouring its way across the country. According to legend, its unique floating feature was actually a production mistake, caused by a P&G employee who left the soap mixer on during his lunch break, allowing for too much air to be mixed into the batch. The aerated bars thus produced had a bouyancy the public loved, and P&G supposedly adopted the technique.

JEEP®

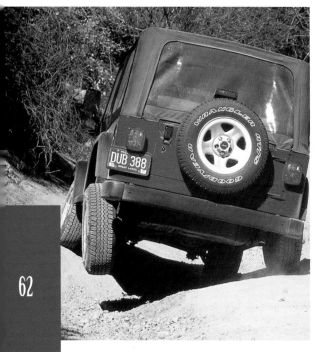

In 1938, as World War II began to flare, the United States Army sent out a memo to car manufacturers, announcing their interest in replacing motorized tricycle sidecars with a lightweight vehicle suitable for reconnaissance missions.

This brief memo triggered a war of its own among car manufacturers. And the Army would confound the issue in July of 1940 by stating that the vehicle had to meet the following specifications: a 1,300-pound total weight, a 660-pound payload capacity, an engine capable of producing 85 pound-feet of torque, a wheelbase not more than 80 inches, and a tread not more than 47 inches. They also asked for a prototype in 49 days and assurance that a shipment of 75 would be available in 70 days.

On September 23, 1940, Bantam emerged in first place with their Blitz Buggy. Granted, the vehicle exceeded the weight requirement by 700 pounds,

4 WHEELER

tipping the scales at considerably less than both the Willys and Ford prototypes. The Army then admitted that its original requirement was unrealistic and reset the limit at 2,100 pounds.

Competing executives, present on that auspicious September morning, immediately returned to their engineers with the new Army requirements and inside info on their competitors' prototypes. A scant six weeks later, Willys-Overland returned with its Quad prototype. Weighing in at 2,100 pounds, seven ounces, it yet offered 105 pound-feet of torque.

The Army, ever the model of diplomacy, ordered 1,500 of each prototype from Bantam, Willys-Overland, and Ford.

Eventually, the Willys-Overland Company yielded the champ with its MA model, which became the MB model in production. This design would soon be known around the world as the Jeep® vehicle. Teamed with Ford's production capacity, they cranked out over 700,000 vehicles during World War II.

The origin of the Jeep brand name is steeped in controversy. Many claim that it derives from the term "General Purpose." (If you slur together the acronym GP, you'll get a sense of how this works.)

However, others argue that the name was born out of none other than E.C. Segar's *Popeye* cartoon. Eugene the Jeep was a heroic, felinelike being who engaged in transdimensional travel. This could explain why the Army painted those Jeep vehicles spinach green.

Each successor to the original 1941 U.S. military Willys MB—from the Jeep CJ-2A to the 1987 Wrangler—improved upon its predecessor's capability and refined its attributes without compromising the authentic Jeep character. Today's Jeep Wrangler is an all-new vehicle, yet it still shares design cues such as the fold-down windshield and the signature Jeep grille and round headlights that are reminiscent of the original Jeep.

JOHN DEERE

The history of John Deere tractors doesn't begin with John Deere at all, but rather involves the story of a man from Froehlich, Iowa, by the name of John Froehlich. No, that's no coincidence. The town was, in fact, named after young John's father.

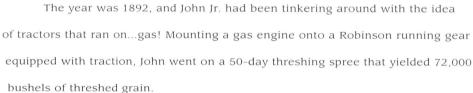

The year was 1892, and John Jr. had been tinkering around with the idea of tractors that ran on...gas! Mounting a gas engine onto a Robinson running gear equipped with traction, John went on a 50-day threshing spree that yielded 72,000 bushels of threshed grain.

One would assume that such a feat would have revolutionized the tractor world; sadly, one would have been mistaken. Enthused by the fruits of his labor, John teamed up with the Waterloo Gasoline Traction Engine Company that same year and sold a whopping two tractors. The following year, both tractors were returned.

This, however, did not deter John or the Waterloo Company, and they set

about reinventing the wheel...literally. By 1897, with the introduction of two new models, sales totaled a promising two; that's not two per unit, but rather two units in sum.

Things were so bad that the Waterloo Gasoline Traction Engine Company began focusing more on stationary engines and soon dropped the word *Traction* from their name. Unfortunately, shortening their name also meant shortening the payroll, for John Froehlich immediately dropped out of the company.

Nevertheless, Froehlich's innovations there had piqued the interest of a group of folks based out of Moline, Illinois, by the name of Deere & Company.

In business since the early 1800s, Deere & Company had recently been experimenting with tractor design and manufacture. They'd built a test pilot that, at the time, was tearing up the Dakotas, but they'd also set their sights on greener pastures.

In 1918, Deere & Company purchased the Waterloo Gasoline Engine Company, and the marriage of ideas, designs, and innovations was a match made in fertile elysian fields. The John Deere Company has since gone on to change the face of agriculture around the globe.

THE JUKEBOX

*A*lthough it didn't exactly qualify as a jukebox, the first known coin-operated music player, traced to a gentleman by the name of Louis Glass, dates back to November 23, 1889. Yes, the very year the Eiffel Tower was erected in Paris, Americans were plugging nickels into Thomas Edison's phonograph, eagerly anticipating their few minutes of acoustical pleasure.

Mr. Glass was a wily entrepreneur whose concept caught on so quickly that within the first week of its installment, his phonograph was earning over $15 a day. By the mid-1890s, the excitement had spread all the way to Europe. Yet, much to Mr. Glass' chagrin, he wasn't able to capitalize further on his ingenuity.

JUKEBOXES

It was the John Gabel Company that, in 1906, introduced the first "jukebox" that offered more than one ditty, calling it the Automatic Entertainer. And it was the advent of radio that made this mode of entertainment a necessary part of every tavern, dance hall, and malt shop throughout the country.

The year 1927 saw the introduction of the Automated Musical Instruments Company's coin-operated 20-song selector. Its rapid popularity gave rise to dozens of imitators, some of which were so untested they scratched records beyond recognition. But a new era was to follow on the heels of the Great Depression.

Two companies tossed their hats into the ring in 1933 and 1935. The first was founded in the 1800s by German emigrant Rudolph Wurlitzer, who had already made strides in the player piano/carousel organ field. The second was Rock-Ola, whose founder was David Rockola.

With all this competition, industry standards drastically increased. Long gone were the days of 20-song selectors. Wall Boxes, as they were often called, were soon capable of 56 musical offerings. And the dull, drab paneling seen on earlier machines quickly gave way to electrified plasticity in every color imaginable.

The 1930s also gave us the word *jukebox*. Myriad tales exist regarding its etymology, but according to Vincent Lynch, author of *American Jukebox: The Classic Years*, the most plausible explanation is that the word *jook* was part of Afro-American slang and meant "dance." *Jook* evolved into *juke*, and the rest, Daddy-O, is history.

LACOSTE

I t was the 1927 Davis Cup Championships at Forest Hills. The U.S. Open Tennis Center in Flushing was just a glimmer in New York's eye. The world waited breathlessly for the French phenom, René "le Crocodile" Lacoste, to step onto the court. Little did the spectators know they were about to observe history being made.

Lacoste made his entrance wearing a short-sleeved shirt! The puritanical tennis dress code of the day called for long-sleeved, woven fabric shirts and long pants. Lacoste's comportment was, simply put, scandalous.

Perhaps René felt that he could get away with it. After all, he had already won Wimbledon and the French Open at Roland Garros Stadium in 1925. The following year he racked up a victory at the U.S. Open, and then won the French and U.S. Opens in 1927. Not only that, but he also led France to their very first Davis Cup victory while wearing his famed shirt.

It was during his Davis Cup performance that the American press labeled Lacoste "le Crocodile." No, it wasn't because he had a croc stitched to his shirt. Rather, this moniker aptly described René's cunning, ruthless style of play.

Interestingly, the shirts did not originally sport the crocodile logo. Rather, they first appeared on René's tennis blazers following his 1927 Forest Hills win. Close friend Robert George seized upon the new epithet and designed the embroidered logo.

It wasn't until a year after Lacoste led his "Musketeers" to their last Davis Cup triumph in 1932 that the piqué knit polo went into production. Doubling up with André Giller, the largest manufacturer of knitwear at that time, Lacoste distributed the shirt only in Europe.

The polos became so popular, however, that by the end of World War II, they were worn by most touring pros and even by those who fit more comfortably in the "hacker" category.

In 1951, the company broadened their spectrum to include other colors and introduced new lines of clothing. During the years that followed, René made numerous contributions to the game of tennis. And, at the time of his death in 1996, he held over 30 patents, including that for Jimmy Connors' weapon of choice, the Wilson T-2000.

LEATHERMAN TOOLS

Beginning his operation in 1983, company president and inventor Tim Leatherman got the inspiration for his Pocket Survival Tool while on a low-budget tour of Europe. It was 1975, and Tim, a self-taught machinist with an engineering background, found himself staying in hotels that weren't exactly five-star. He was forced to rely on his trusty camper's knife to get himself out of plumbing jams. Unfortunately, it didn't prove all too useful in such situations. What Tim really needed was some sort of pocket tool box.

Upon his return, Tim partnered up with friend Steve Berliner. After eight tireless years of designing and redesigning, endeavoring to make their device more compact, Tim and Steve struck oil in 1983.

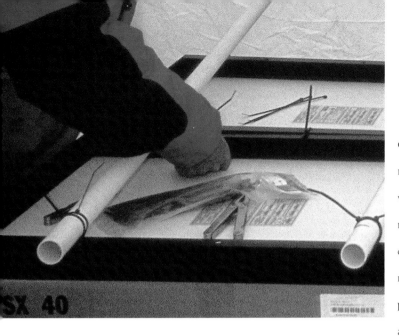

SX 40

Setting up shop in Portland, Oregon, the Leatherman Tool Group made their entrance into the market with the Pocket Survival Tool. This miraculous all-in-one invention contained needlenose pliers; regular pliers; wire cutters; a clip point knife; metal and wood files; a ruler; can and bottle openers; small, medium, and large screwdrivers; a Phillips screwdriver; and an awl/punch. And it weighed a mere five ounces.

It was no surprise, then, when this handy little pocket tool's popularity spread like wildfire. Letters began pouring in from around the country from campers, outdoorspeople, and adventurers whose lives had been literally saved by the Pocket Survival Tool.

In one testimonial, an aviator's single-engine plane was sure to crash into the Alaska Range when the landing gear failed. Seconds before impact, he pried open the instrument panel with his Leatherman and used his needlenose pliers to fish out the broken cable. The landing gear released, and both pilot and passenger were saved.

Tim has since expanded the line, and Leatherman now offers five different Pocket Survival Tools. In addition to the original, with 12 essential tools in one, there's the PST II™, which adds scissors, a file with diamond coating, and a unique sharpening groove. The bigger, stronger Super Tool™ has 10 locking blades with 18 total features, including saw, serrated knife blade, electrical crimper, and wire stripper. Conversely, the Mini-Tool™ is a mere $2^5/_8$ inches long, yet in seconds becomes a full-size pair of pliers. Finally, the newest Leatherman is the Micra™, which is designed to give you the best possible scissors in a tiny 2.5-inch package that weighs only 1.75 ounces.

Recently, a Leatherman made its first recorded ascent up Mount Everest. Pretty impressive for a tool that owes its origins to faulty plumbing!

71

LEICA

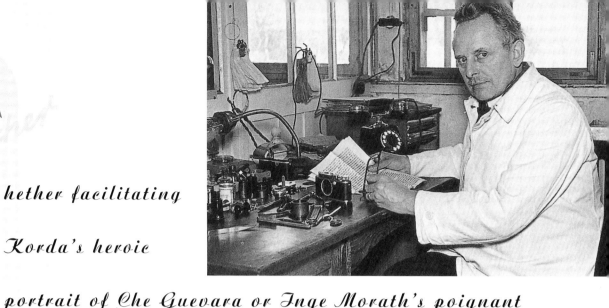

*W*hether facilitating Korda's heroic portrait of Che Guevara or Inge Morath's poignant glimpse of Marilyn Monroe during the filming of <u>The Misfits</u> or Eddie Adams' shocking documentation of a Vietnamese police chief shooting a suspected Viet Cong point-blank, Leica cameras have captured some of the most hallowed and harrowing moments of the 20th century.

It all started in 1911, when a mechanical engineer by the name of Oskar Barnack was hired by Ernst Leitz to assist in the research department of Leitz's company in Wetzlar, Germany. An avid amateur photographer interested in movie camera technology, Oskar was already working on ways to reduce the bulkiness of the heavy-plated cameras of the time.

After three years, Oskar hit upon the concept of doubling the current movie film format for use as photographic material. This new format became known as 35mm and forever changed the course of modern photography.

What's fascinating is that it was not at all what Oskar was hired to do. In fact, the early development of Leica cameras was accomplished in his spare time.

In any case, the year 1914 saw Barnack's first 35mm pictures, which were taken with what was then called the Ur-Leica. Unfortunately, the First World War was raging in Europe, and the idea of celebrating the moments of our lives took somewhat of a backseat.

By 1920, following a cease-fire in the conflict, the Leitz Company took more of an interest in Barnack's innovation. In fact, one of the very first photo news reports was taken that year by Barnack himself, witness to the great floods of Wetzlar.

Just five years later, at the Leipzig Spring Fair, pocket-sized Leicas were unleashed on a skeptical public. Perhaps because brilliance is often first met with resistance, professional photographers deemed the camera too small to be taken seriously. Besides, where was the tripod?

The Leitz Company, however, was not deterred. Over the course of the next 29 years, they improved upon each successive model, their work culminating in 1954 with the introduction of the world-famous Leica M3.

Originally conceived in 1936, the M3 did not make its entrance into the market until 1954 due to the Second World War. In fact, the design had been sitting in a desk drawer for nearly 10 years before it was discovered.

With its bayonet mount for interchangeable lenses, brightline viewfinder showing image area in the finder, rapid film advance lever, film counter with automatic reset, and countless other features, the M3 quickly became the preferred camera of photographers from Henri Cartier-Bresson to Mary Ellen Mark to Sebastião Salgado.

LEVI STRAUSS

It was the Gold Rush of 1849, and ambitious Americans were packing up their families and making the long trek to the Wild West.

Prospectors were so anxious to stake their claim that many left with only the clothes on their backs—no tents, no luggage, no nothin'. One of these pioneers ultimately decided to leave the mining to others more inclined, for his gold-digging would take a road much less traveled.

An emigrant tailor from Germany, Levi Strauss, ventured forth to find his fortune armed only with a supply of needles, thread, and canvas. His plan, ironically, had nothing to with creating garments. Rather, he figured that most clothing wouldn't stand up to the rigors of the West, so there'd be plenty of darning to do. And, as a side venture, he'd use his load of canvas to make tents to house the miners.

Upon his arrival, threadbare prospectors couldn't care less about the state of their garments, nor were they interested in buying tents. Things started looking bleak for Strauss, but before he could put down his needle and pick up a mining pan, he received a challenge at a local saloon.

A miner wagered that Strauss couldn't make a pair of trousers that would withstand the punishing conditions of the trade. Remembering the hundreds of yards of unsold canvas he possessed, Levi took the man up on his bet. Thus, in 1850 was born the first pair of Levi's "waist-high overalls."

His dirt-brown pants became a much-coveted item in California, but Levi soon ran out of canvas. Because overseas shipments took far too long, he needed to find a more accessible, equally durable material. Providence availed itself in the form of a cotton-woven fabric being produced in New Hampshire.

Originally from France, the fabric, called serge de Nimes, was named after the town in which it was produced. Eventually, the serge was dropped, leaving only de Nimes. This denim fabric was apparently first used by sailors from the Italian port of Genoa or, as it is pronounced *en français*, Genes. And such is the etymology of "denim jeans."

Strauss ordered bulk shipments of this fabric, which turned out not to be dirt brown like the original canvas pants, but rather were stained with a bluish indigo dye. Since the 17th century, producers of denim had traditionally dyed it blue. And what was good enough for the French was certainly good enough for us. Since then, over 2.5 billion pairs of Levi's blue jeans have been sold.

J E A N S

LIONEL TRAINS

When Joshua Lionel Cowen came forth with his first patent, he imagined his career in photography would be well under way. It was 1899, and he had just invented a method by which flash powder could be ignited by using dry cell batteries to heat a wire fuse. At any moment, Eastman Kodak was sure to call.

Suddenly, there was a knock at the door. Standing before him was an admiral from the U.S. Navy. A bit puzzled by the military interest, Cowen answered the summons to demonstrate his invention in Washington.

As it turns out, the Navy didn't want to take pictures in the dark. Rather, they were blown away by the miniature detonation device Joshua had fashioned. They conferred for a moment and then offered him a $12,000 contract to develop his process for electrically charged mine detonation.

Cowen returned to his home base in the Lower East Side of Manhattan, hired an assistant, and began to fulfill his end of the contract. Although destruction wasn't exactly what he'd had in mind, $12,000 was big money in 1899.

Having fulfilled his obligation to the Navy, Cowen took his earnings and, in September of 1900, opened the Lionel Manufacturing Company, makers of "electrical novelties." The idea of crafting electric trains had yet to enter his mind. In fact, he would tinker with inventing the electric fan and the flashlight before he got himself on track.

The following year, after noticing a toy and novelty display in the window of Ingersoll's, Cowen experienced an "aha" moment. The poor playthings sat lifeless, devoid of excitement. Wouldn't it help attract business if the displays presented continual motion?

Cowen raced back to his shop and set to work. Beginning with a rectangular wooden box, he affixed the motor from his failed fan invention, attached insulated metal wheels, constructed a metal track set in wooden ties, and wired dry cell batteries right into the track. He then stained the wooden box red and stenciled on it *Electric Express*.

Cowen ran back to the toy store to present this new sales tool. Greatly impressed, Ingersoll immediately placed it in the window. Soon, passersby crowded the store window, struggling to catch sight of the miraculous miniature train. But instead of Ingersoll's merchandise, they wanted to buy the actual display. And with that, Lionel trains were on their way, full steam ahead.

LOUISVILLE SLUGGER

*I*t was 1884, and a local woodworker named Bud Hillerich constructed a brand-new bat for Pete "The Old Gladiator" Browning, star of Louisville's very own Eclipse. This new stick was called the Falls City Slugger. Ten years later, Hillerich swapped "Falls City" for "Louisville," and the family business was well under way.

Now, the sport of baseball was the national pastime, and many bats were already being manufactured by companies with greater experience. How did this rookie company win its way into baseball equipment's clean-up spot?

According to John Monteleone and Mark Gola, who wrote *The Louisville Slugger Ultimate Book of Hitting*, baseball bat manufacturers weren't exactly personalizing their products at the time. They cranked out plenty of product but seldom customized bats to players' specifications.

Not so for Hillerich, who took into account each player's preference for weight, length, and style. And, upon completion of each Louisville Slugger, he not only branded the bats with their trademark but also carved in that particular player's name.

Into its 113th year as the preferred weapon of choice by major leaguers from San Francisco to Bean Town, the manufacturing of Louisville Sluggers has been turned into a veritable science by the Hillerich & Bradsby Company. In fact, from the moment that a white ash is harvested from either Pennsylvania or New York, it's a solid eight-week process before a bat can even get written into the lineup.

Oh, but the wait is well worth it! It seems that every star of the diamond has relied upon his trusty Louisville Slugger to secure his place in the Baseball Hall of Fame in Cooperstown, New York—from Golden Agers Honus Wagner, Ty Cobb, and Lou Gehrig to Mickey Mantle, Joe DiMaggio, and Jackie Robinson to Willie Mays, Hank Aaron, and Reggie Jackson to would-be Hall of Famers Cal Ripken Jr., Ken Griffey Jr., and Mike Piazza.

But lest you think we've forgotten the Rajah of Rap, the Maharajah of Mash, the Caliph of Clout, the Behemoth of Bust, the Sultan of Swing, the one, the only Bambino, the Babe—George Herman Ruth—we haven't. Brandishing his 54-ounce Louisville "beast," the Babe accounted for 148 of his remarkable 714 round-trippers in just his first few seasons in Yankee pinstripes. A legendary bat for a legend of the game.

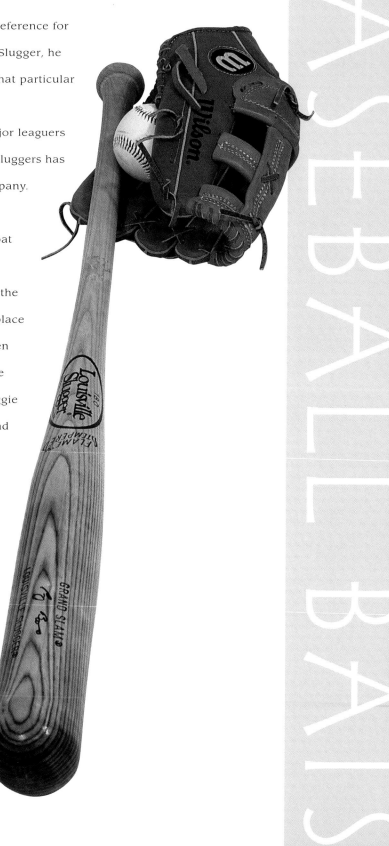

LOUIS VUITTON

In 1837, a 14-year-old boy arrived in Paris after an arduous 250-mile trek. His name was Louis Vuitton, and his elegant designs would soon leave an indelible impression on the travel and leisure industry.

After several years as an apprentice to a Parisian trunk-maker who specialized in packing hoopskirts and ball gowns for the aristocracy, Vuitton acquired an unusual reputation: Elaborate crinoline gowns that he packed for long overseas journeys somehow arrived with nary a wrinkle.

By 1853, Vuitton's abilities became so widely acclaimed that none other than Empress Eugenie, wife of Napoleon, hired him to be her exclusive dress-packer. He opened his very first shop in Paris the following year. In addition to servicing his aristocratic clientele, he returned to his first love: designing trunks.

After persuading the founder of the General Transatlantic Company to show him the designs for the cargo holds on the new fleet of passenger ships, Vuitton realized that the typical

dome-shaped trunk was not practical for stowing, and it would be simpler if the new breed of trunks was flat-topped and easily stackable. As a result, he created the very first flat trunk, thus securing his place in luggage history.

The Vuitton tradition of quality and excellence has been well maintained. Louis' son, Georges, followed ably in his father's footsteps. In 1896, he patented the famous Vuitton monogram design. He also invented the "unpickable" five-tumbler personalized lock that is an integral feature of every Vuitton suitcase.

George's son, Gaston, further revolutionized the industry in 1959 by developing a new coating process that led to the introduction of today's renowned soft luggage in the Monogram canvas.

Over the years, the Vuitton family has handcrafted cases for such notables as the Duke and Duchess of Windsor, Coco Chanel, Charles Lindbergh, Douglas Fairbanks, Mary Pickford, the Aga Khan, and Ernest Hemingway.

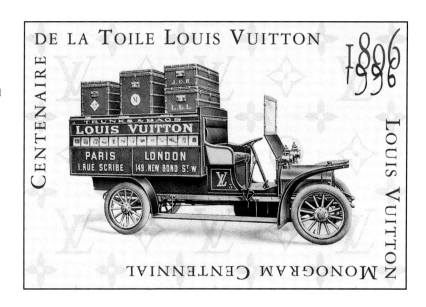

LUCCHESE

*D*eep in the heart of Texas, near the banks of the Rio Grande, are found a group of craftsmen known world-wide for masterful boot making. But at their El Paso location on Montana Avenue, you're not apt to hear the names Tex, Bucky, or Hoss bandied about. You've stepped into Lucchese country.

Before the outbreak of the Civil War, six brothers left their native Italy and immigrated to America. Arriving in San Antonio, one of the brothers, Samuel Lucchese, known throughout Italy for his boot-making skills, decided to start up a business.

After several years of modest success, during which he won the respect of soldiers from nearby Fort Sam Houston as well as the admiration of ranchers and cowboys of the Wild West, Samuel took his brothers in as partners. They would soon open their doors to a wider-reaching public.

The very first Lucchese Bros. Manufacturers of Boots & Shoes outlet appeared in 1883. And although their reputation for soft, supple

B O O T S

leather-hide boots was spreading far and wide, the company lacked that certain something that would lift them, soaring, into the 20th century. Enter Samuel's son, Cosimo.

Shortly before 1920, Cosimo joined the company and, for the first time in family history, began to actively market their product. The results were astounding, as cowgirls, cowboys, and wanna-be's flocked to Texas for a chance to slip into a pair of real American folklore.

In the 1950s, Cosimo's son, Sam, followed in his father's bootsteps to administer further breakthroughs in marketing.

Since that time, the Lucchese client list has read like a Who's Who of Hollywood. John Wayne, Lorne Greene, Lloyd Bridges, Jimmy Stewart, Gary Cooper, and Gregory Peck—not to mention those legends of the Wild West, Abbott & Costello and Zsa Zsa Gabor—have stepped into the boots that helped blaze the trail of Western expansion.

Those who will settle for nothing but the best can don a pair of Lucchese boots in a variety of styles—and prices. The western-style boots start at $450 for basic calf and goat leather and go up to $6,000 for full alligator, with those made from Taju lizard, ostrich, anteater, and South African python (all from farmed animals) falling somewhere in between. The West may have already been won, but you can still dress the part.

MANISCHEWITZ

Old Testament 101. When Moses led his exodus of enslaved people out of Egypt, they did not have time to allow their bread to rise. This unleavened bread, or matzo, baked to a thin crisp by the hot desert sun, became a symbol of the struggle for freedom celebrated by the Passover holiday.

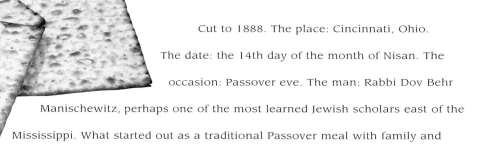

Cut to 1888. The place: Cincinnati, Ohio. The date: the 14th day of the month of Nisan. The occasion: Passover eve. The man: Rabbi Dov Behr Manischewitz, perhaps one of the most learned Jewish scholars east of the Mississippi. What started out as a traditional Passover meal with family and friends ended in a series of events that many would never forget.

MATZO

Experimenting with gas-fired ovens instead of the commonly used black-iron coal stoves of the day, Rabbi Dov Behr baked a truly delectable matzo. The rabbi, while pleased with his family's response, had no desire to take this any further. But the Manischewitz clan insisted. And that very same year, the first matzo bakery was established in that sleepy Ohio River town.

Once the company's doors opened to the public, Rabbi Dov Behr demonstrated himself to be a man of great integrity. He apparently had no interest in building a phenomenally successful business. Instead, he was concerned with creating a company whose ideals perpetuated the sacred laws of kashruth, or Jewish dietary laws.

Nevertheless, demand was so great that Rabbi Dov Behr responded with an unrivaled brilliance and innovation. He perfected his gas-fired oven process, which led to a controlled baking operation. In addition, he created the traveling oven and was the first to package matzos for distribution outside his neighborhood.

The name Manischewitz has since come to stand for such a high level of quality and excellence that companies eagerly seek the opportunity to license the name, confident that the association will help them gain acceptance even in non-Jewish homes.

Now, three generations later, Manischewitz products are a family favorite throughout the world. Aside from matzo, these products include a stunning array of kosher comestibles ranging from gefilte fish to wine to borscht to (what else?) chicken soup.

MARTINIS

*I*t's nearly impossible to conceive of this nectar of sophisticates without evoking the poster child for high society, Bond...James Bond. Only the inimitable Mr. Bond could so nonchalantly turn toward a barman and request a martini shaken...not stirred. So chic, so suave, so debonair. However, this "finest of all cocktails" actually pre-dates 007 by more than half a century.

According to Michael Jackson's reliable *Bar & Cocktail Companion: The Connoisseur's Handbook*, the martini originated in the swellegant year of 1910 in New York City's swank Knickerbocker Hotel.

There was a bartender by the name of...yes, Martini...who was handed the daunting responsibility of coming up with a new beverage for John D. Rockefeller. The drink consisted of disproportionate parts of gin and vermouth.

It's unknown the ratio Martini concocted, but Jackson looks to authority John Doxat, who suggests the ideal blend is as follows:

Begin with a hint of dry vermouth; pour 4 ounces into a mixing glass filled with ice; then before it can even get comfortable in its new digs, drain out the liquid and drizzle in 2 ounces of gin. Stir not too vigorously for a half a minute, then pour into (what else?) a martini glass. This will leave you holding a classic 1:11 martini. Garnish according to taste with either lemon rind or olive.

Since that fateful day in 1910, martinis have dazzled the palates of many of society's luminaries. One can just imagine Dorothy Parker taking a tantalizing pull off of her martini while leering seductively at Robert Benchley sitting across from her at the Algonquin Round Table.

Or who can forget Hawkeye Pierce and Trapper John's relentless quest for the perfect dry martini in episode after episode of "M*A*S*H"? In fact, one show had Hawkeye suggesting that the perfect blend involved drinking straight gin while staring at a picture of the man responsible for creating vermouth. Many would tend to agree.

But what about James Bond's Martini technique? Well, according to any mixologist worth his salt, a shaken martini runs the risk of "bruising" the gin and damaging the full flavor. Conventional wisdom recommends that one mingle the ingredients tenderly for optimum effect.

MICHELIN

In 1889, a bicyclist with a punctured tire stopped at a modest rubber products factory managed by Edouard Michelin in the town of Clermont Ferrard, France. The punctured tire, like tires of the day, was glued to the rim. Edouard, while repairing the tire, recognized the enormous potential for demountable bicycle tires. So he set to work on a design. A few weeks later, he took out a patent for a detachable tire which could be repaired in minutes rather than hours.

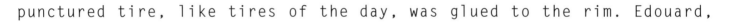

Just six years later, in 1895, Edouard introduced the world's first pneumatic tires for automobiles. A car, built by Michelin with a Peugeot chassis, was dubbed "Eclair" and driven by Edouard and his brother Andrew in the famed Paris to Bordeaux to Paris road race. It was one of the earliest of a long list of innovations in a proud Michelin history.

MICHELIN®

Interestingly, the congenial Michelin Man was created three years later in 1898, when the brothers were attending a trade show in Lyon, France. Spotting a stack of tires, Edouard commented, "If it had arms and legs, it would look like a man." Hence the introduction of Bibendum®, also known as the Michelin Man.

The name Bibendum is actually derived from a poster in which he is seen holding up a goblet filled with stones, nails, and broken glass. The caption declares, "Nunc est Bibendum!" And the name stuck.

In 1946, Michelin broke seemingly impenetrable ground with the radial tire. The tire takes its name from the reinforcing cords which run at "radial," or 90-degree, angles to the wheel. It doubled the tread mileage compared with conventional crossply tires and measurably enhanced the handling and cornering. The radial tire set a standard of quality and excellence that changed the power structure among major tire manufacturers and clearly established Michelin as a major force in the industry.

Today, Michelin manufactures and sells tires for every type of vehicle—from bicycles to cars; from trucks to the space shuttle. A century of firsts includes introducing steel into tires; the low-profile tire; the 80,000-mile tire; and the first 700,000-mile truck tire warranty. And Michelin is still setting standards with products like the ZP zero-pressure tire that will not go flat.

Clearly, the revolution that began 50 years ago continues as Michelin retains its pioneering leadership title.

MONTBLANC

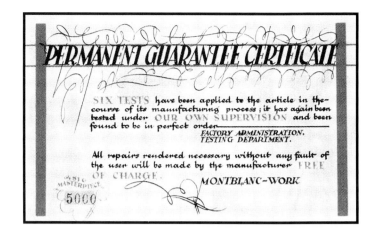

PERMANENT GUARANTEE CERTIFICATE

SIX TESTS have been applied to the article in the course of its manufacturing process; it has again been tested under OUR OWN SUPERVISION and been found to be in perfect order.
FACTORY ADMINISTRATION.
TESTING DEPARTMENT.

All repairs rendered necessary without any fault of the user will be made by the manufacturer FREE OF CHARGE.
MONTBLANC-WORK

5000

*T*he idea for the Montblanc, the world's premier writing instrument, started when August Eberstein, a German technical engineer who studied fountain pen design in the United States and England, returned to Berlin to start his own business with a merchant named Alfred Nehemias.

Bessie Wallace Kgl. Württ. Hofschauspielerin, als Montblanc-Füllhalter von der Firma L.Schaller, beim Theaterball Stuttgart 1914

In 1906, listing themselves in the Berlin Commercial Directory under the exceedingly lengthy name of Gold Fountain Pen Factory Simplo Filler Pen Company, the two men created a pen that bore the moniker Rouge et Noir.

This beautiful, stylish pen was well received. However, while stationers swooned, investors shied away, and shortly after the commencement of their endeavor, August Eberstein withdrew from the operation.

Nehemias, on the other hand, knew that their creation was too important to forgo. He contacted an entrepreneur in Hamburg by the name of Claus Johannes

Voss, who, along with his associate Max Koch, provided enough funding to bring Eberstein out of retirement. By the end of 1908, the foursome was well on its way to redefining the gentle art of handwriting.

It was during a hot game of skat in 1910 that a family member of one of the partners boldly drew an analogy between the pen, which had become the pinnacle of writing instruments, and the majestic Mont Blanc, which is the highest peak in the Alps. Overnight, the pen, as well as the company, adopted the new name, one that truly does inspire artists to strive toward wondrous heights.

So impressed were the creators with this new association that the plain white pen's cap was transformed into a visualizaton of an aerial view of Mont Blanc's snow-capped peak. And in 1924, with the introduction of the newest Montblanc pen—the formidable Meisterstück 149—Eberstein and company took this one step further. Hand-etched into the 18-kt. gold nib of each pen is the bird's-eye view of snow-covered Mont Blanc as well as the cryptic number 4,810 (the actual height in meters of the Mont Blanc peak). Today the Meisterstück 149 is considered the most celebrated writing instrument of all time.

P E N S

MONTECRISTO

*H*avanas. The crème de la crème of the cigar world. But ask any aficionado, from the shores of Cuba to the burnished-oak smoking parlors of London, and they'll tell you that the Montecristo is the greatest cigar of all time. Actually, the Montecristo No. 2, to be more precise.

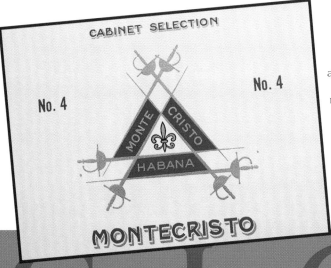

Although first hand-rolled in 1934, Montecristo is still perceived as the new kid on the Havana block. In fact, they are one of only two manufacturers of Cuban cigars to begin their operations in the 20th century and still be in existence today.

The company name derives from the Alexandre Dumas classic *The Count of Monte Cristo*, in which the count is described as such: "I think he is an excellent host, that he has traveled much, and...he has

CIGARS

some excellent cigars." (It's not known how "Monte Cristo" transformed into "Montecristo.")

Since their entrance into the cigar-smoking world, Montecristos have set the standard by which all Cuban brands are judged. They are so sought after that counterfeiters have been peddling knockoffs worldwide for nearly as long as the company's been in business.

Consumers often fall victim to forgers, and for a novice it's difficult to detect a fake from the verité, but here's a quick tip: Many counterfeiters have been known to print up elaborate labels bearing the famed six-crossed-swords pattern, only to have the name read "Monte Cristo."

There exists another Montecristo cigar, which is manufactured in the Dominican Republic. While this blend enjoys a fine reputation, it is in no way associated with its Cuban counterpart. In fact, when Fidel Castro nationalized the factories in Cuba, many cigar-makers fled, taking their brand names with them. Romeo y Julieta and Cohiba are among other Havanas that have Dominican namesakes.

Now well into its 63rd year, Montecristo is known by many to be the ultimate "power smoke." And although they are not currently found at local American tobacconists due to a trade embargo, they can be purchased abroad—for a price. In Switzerland, for example, a box of the coveted cigars sells for around $200. And the lengths to which some will go in order to secure even one is astounding. Many international travelers passing through U.S. Customs fear those dreaded words, "Have you anything to declare?"

OREO COOKIES

To dunk or not to dunk? That is the question. Well, if one dunks, then one is unable to twist apart the chocolate wafers, thereby missing out on the time-honored tradition of scraping off the creme center with one's teeth. Such a dilemma!

Cookies have been around for what seems like forever. But Oreos can lay claim to being the most famous cookie of all time.

Yet, sadly, no one, not even its creator, Nabisco, can say how or why the Oreo came to be so named. Several theories prevail. One derives from the cookies' original hill-like shape; in Greek, the word for "mountain" is *oreo*. Then there's the idea that the early Oreo packages had a gold color, and *or* being the French word for "gold," plus *eo*?

There are those who maintain that the name originated from the "melodic combination of sounds with just a few catch letters and it was easy to pronounce." Whatever the source, Oreo need not explain

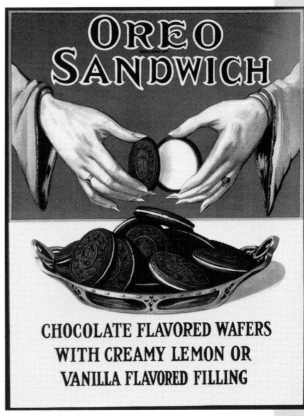

itself, thanks to overwhelming acceptance since its introduction in 1913.

But how, you may wonder, did these sweet and petite sandwiches become so successful? Start with two chocolate wafers made from the purest Dutch cocoa, garnish with an iced vanilla creme filling, then try to eat just one.

Over the years, Oreos have secured their place in the cookie hall of fame. So popular is the original recipe that Nabisco bakeries produce literally millions of these 1³/₄-inch-diameter babies in a single eight-hour shift.

And, for those left unsatisfied by a dollop of creme, why not make it a double? Since its debut in 1975, the Oreo Double Stuf is considered the fifth most successful cookie in history.

And for those feeling particularly decadent, there is the fudge-covered Double Stuf.

PERRIER

Approximately 130 million years ago, snuggled within the Cretaceous Era, an event occurred in an area that would eventually become known as France. A particular limestone deposit formed faults and fissures so configured that water trapped within the earth's core resurfaced with a pleasing carbonated effervescence. Who could predict that eons later, connoisseurs the world over would request this water by name: Perrier?

The source of Perrier, known within the industry as Source Perrier, is nestled in the fertile crescent of Vergeze, in Provence, an area in the south of France. According to the Perrier Group's *Perrier Primer*:

"Rain travels through layers of porous limestone, cracked marl (a hard, claylike rock rich in calcium carbonate), and pure white

sand (which sustains the water's clarity), and the water is naturally filtered as it acquires the minerals which give Perrier its own character and good taste.

Nature provides added protection with an 8–15 foot layer of impermeable

clay which surrounds the source for over a mile in all directions, guarding it from any surface contaminants." The carbonation, meanwhile, comes from volcanic gases trapped within the geologic strata that rise and mingle with the water.

Humankind's first encounter with this premier refreshment is thought to date back to 218 B.C., when Hannibal's Carthaginian Army paused at what was apparently the world's very first rest stop.

Nearly 2000 years later, a gentleman by the name of Dr. Perrier, who set about "developing the source," offered a thirst-quenching sip to Napoleon III. The emperor was so impressed that he immediately decreed that Perrier be bottled "for the good of France."

Shortly thereafter, one of the early owners of the company, Sir John Harmsworth, suffered an injury that forced him to pursue rehabilitation involving large wooden clubs. On a whim, he determined that Perrier be packaged in bottles fashioned after those clubs. Herein lies the tale of "Earth's First Soft Drink."

MINERAL WATER

PEZ®

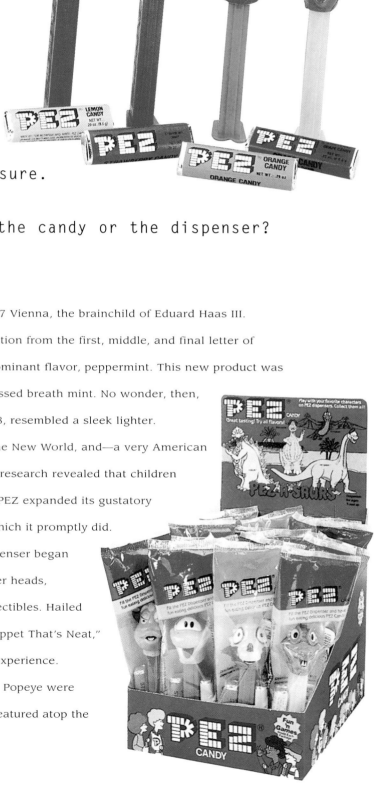

PEZ. An international

candy culture. A

transgenerational treasure.

But which came first, the candy or the dispenser?

PEZ candy first appeared in 1927 Vienna, the brainchild of Eduard Haas III. Haas concocted the name for his confection from the first, middle, and final letter of PfeffErminZ, the German word for its dominant flavor, peppermint. This new product was marketed to adult smokers as a compressed breath mint. No wonder, then, that the first dispenser, debuting in 1948, resembled a sleek lighter.

In 1952, PEZ found its way to the New World, and—a very American thing to do—it reinvented itself. Market research revealed that children would respond more enthusiastically if PEZ expanded its gustatory spectrum to fruit flavors—which it promptly did.

Also promptly, the dispenser began sporting famed character heads, destined to become collectibles. Hailed as "A Treat to Eat in a Puppet That's Neat," PEZ redefined the candy experience.

Mickey Mouse and Popeye were two of the first characters featured atop the

dispensers. Rare designs such as those from the psychedelic series of the 1960s, which included the psychedelic eye and the psychedelic flower, are the envy of today's collectors. Yet of the many hundreds of varieties of PEZ dispensers sold through the years, that venerable icon, Santa Claus, has remained No. 1 on the market.

Forty-five or so years after hitting America, more than 1 billion PEZ are sold annually in the USA. And, PEZ continue to be consumed around the globe; in fact, some candy flavors are available only in certain locales. Want a bite of an apple PEZ? Take a plane to Spain. Craving a chocolate PEZ? Head for Hungary or Thailand. Available dispensers also depend on geography. Walt Disney's Huey, Dewey, and Louie may be sold in Canada, but not in the United States.

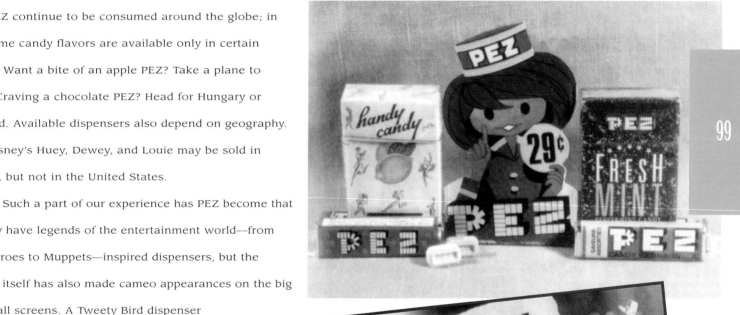

Such a part of our experience has PEZ become that not only have legends of the entertainment world—from superheroes to Muppets—inspired dispensers, but the product itself has also made cameo appearances on the big and small screens. A Tweety Bird dispenser played a pivotal role in a "Seinfeld" episode, and an Elvis Presley dispenser popped up in the film *The Client*, starring Tommy Lee Jones and Susan Sarandon. But don't try to find that Elvis collectible at your local drugstore; it was created specially for the movie.

POLAROID

Edward Land, a Harvard student nearing the close of his freshman year in 1926, found himself agonizing over the following dilemma: "Do I continue on to my sophomore year, or do I drop out and pursue independent research on polarization?"

Fortunately for all, he chose the untrodden trail that led to the invention of the Polaroid camera.

Edward promptly beat a path for New York City. In less than three years, he had created a prototype for his synthetic polarizer. He then returned to the ivied walls and hallowed halls of Harvard.

There, he teamed up with a young physicist named George Wheelwright III. Edward's thesis was that because polarizing materials screened light, they could block the light waves that cause glare. The two men founded the Land-Wheelwright

CAMERAS

Laboratories, and by 1934, they had received a patent for their polarization process.

Although this did not immediately lead to the creation of the Polaroid camera, the business did stay afloat through 1935 thanks to Eastman Kodak, which used Land-Wheelwright's polarizing materials to cut down on glare in photos. Two years later, after a friend had dubbed the process Polaroid, Edward formed the Polaroid Corporation. In 1940, Edward bought out George, who signed up for the Navy and shipped himself out to sea...and away from Land.

By the early 1940s, Land found himself in dire straits. Then along came Christmas 1943. Edward and his wife took scads of photos of their three-year-old opening up her presents. When the dear tot asked to see the undeveloped pictures right away, the bulb flashed in her dad's head, and he hit upon the idea of self-developing film.

While the Polaroid Corporation busily researched the concept, Land brashly promised that he would unveil the camera to the world in February of the following year. His researchers worked around the clock, and on February 21, 1947, Land snapped a photo of himself, pulled back the negative, and one minute later, there his likeness stood.

The *New York Times*, which was on the scene, made Mr. Land front-page news. By the end of the year, the first Polaroids were being sold at the Boston department store Jordan Marsh. Tipping the scale at over five pounds, they cost $89.75 each (film not included). All 56 units sold out that day, and before anyone could say "Cheese," Polaroid had become an institution.

POLO

"*When I design, I create a world. I imagine every detail—the place, the man, the woman. What they are doing, what they are wearing, right down to the fragrance.*"

If you're smelling something pleasant and you can't eat it, there's a good chance it was designed by Ralph Lauren. Polo was created by Lauren in 1978 and is one of the most popular men's scents around the world, evoking the masculine tradition of wood, leather, and tobacco. As Polo fragrance celebrates its 20th anniversary, it is consistently a favorite among men of all ages. Is there any man who has never given or received a gift of Polo? The scent still ranks in the top 10 in department stores and is a perennial best seller at Father's Day and other holidays.

Polo is the original fragrance that embodies the world of Ralph Lauren, and it is just one example of the quality and elegance that epitomize the designer's creations. Since he first introduced Polo men's ties in 1967, Mr. Lauren's work has come to represent the best of American design.

The world of Polo Ralph Lauren for men includes the Purple Label Collection, Polo Ralph Lauren, Polo Sport, Double RL, and Chaps. Ralph Lauren Womenswear, launched in 1981, now encompasses his signature Collection, Collection Classics, RALPH, Ralph Lauren Polo Sport, and Lauren. His fashion collections span from footwear to sleepwear, underwear, swimwear, hosiery, hats, gloves, jewelry, scarves, eyewear, leathergoods, handbags, luggage, and clothing for infants and toddlers. The Ralph Lauren Home Collection premiered in 1983 and includes furniture, linens, and paint.

Ralph Lauren has also created an outstanding wardrobe of fragrances—grooming and skin fitness products for men and women—each conjuring a distinctive mood: Polo, Lauren, Safari, Safari for Men, Polo Crest, Polo Sport, and Ralph Lauren Polo Sport Woman. Each fragrance is an award-winner, earning numerous prizes from the Fragrance Foundation.

Mr. Lauren's first store opened in 1981 and eventually led to his gracious New York City flagship store in the former Rhinelander Mansion on Madison Avenue, which debuted in 1986. In 1993, the Polo Sport store opened directly across the street, featuring modern activewear. Mr. Lauren's international presence includes shops in London, Tokyo, and Paris, and today there are 114 Polo/Ralph Lauren stores around the world.

Throughout his career, Ralph Lauren has received numerous accolades for his impact on style and culture, including several awards from the Council of Fashion Designers of America: 1996 Menswear Designer of the Year, 1995 Womenswear Designer of the Year, and the 1992 Lifetime Achievement Award.

Of all his achievements, however, Mr. Lauren is especially proud of his leadership in philanthropic causes near to his heart. In 1989, Mr. Lauren launched the Nina Hyde Center for Breast Cancer initiative; in 1996, Princess Diana presented Ralph Lauren with the first Humanitarian Award from the Nina Hyde Center. Mr. Lauren also co-chaired the CFDA's New York 7th on Sale benefits in 1990 and 1995, which combined raised more than $10 million toward AIDS research and education.

103

COLOGNE

RAY-BAN SUNGLASSES

BALORAMA

In 1852, German immigrant John Jacob Bausch embarked on a venture to sell European optical imports in his adopted town of Rochester, New York. Not long after, Henry Lomb spotted his pal a $60 business loan. In turn, John made Henry a partner, changing the company name to Bausch & Lomb.

The launch of Bausch & Lomb fortuitously coincided with the invention of Vulcanite. Fashioning eyeglass frames out of this hard rubber, the partners fitted them with European lenses. This put Bausch & Lomb on the map and enabled John to focus on continuing to develop lens applications.

In the ensuing years, B&L made binoculars, telescopes, and microscopes, culminating with Bausch's son William's 1912 invention of optical quality glass. The U.S. Army promptly commissioned the manufacture of lenses for field glasses, rifle scopes, and searchlights. Then the Depression hit.

SUNGLASSES

Despite the bleak economic climate, business boomed for Bausch & Lomb. They won another Army contract, this time to develop sunglasses for Army pilots that would cut down on glare. B&L responded with the appropriately named Anti-Glares. The eyeglasses were a hit with pilots, and by 1936, Bausch & Lomb had renamed the sunglasses Ray-Ban and put them on the market.

The following year, the company launched their all-time best-seller Aviator glasses. In case you need a visual, think Tom Cruise in the 1986 flick *Top Gun*. But this wasn't the first pair of Ray-Ban sunglasses that Mr. Cruise would help immortalize.

In 1953, before Tom was even a glimmer in his mother's eye, the Ray-Ban Wayfarer sunglass graced the visages of some of the country's heppest cats. Priced at $7.50, the classic design won immediate success, but nearly 30 years later, sales suddenly went through the roof, courtesy of Hollywood.

In a movie called *Risky Business*, Cruise played a straight-laced high school kid who loosens up while his parents are out of town. During the course of his matriculation into the world of hip-dom, he latches on to a pair of black Wayfarers, thereby redefining "cool" for millions of teens and 20-somethings around the world. Since then, Ray-Ban has been the preferred sunglass choice of Hollywood, playing a featured role in such films as *Jerry McGuire*, *Broken Arrow*, *Men in Black* and the upcoming release of *Blues Brothers 2000*.

RIVA AQUARAMA

*F*ade in. The Mediterranean. A twin-engine speedboat skips across a sea of relentless whitecaps. Behind the wheel is Sean Connery. Beside him sits Ursula Andress, gently shaking a sterling silver tumbler filled with rocks, gin, and just a whisper of vermouth. Danger may well lurk, but Sean and Ursula are fabulously nonchalant as their Riva Aquarama spirits them to safety.

In its 35-year history, the Riva Aquarama has become known as the playboy's (or -girl's) play toy, the aristocrat's accoutrement, the ultimate impulse purchase.

In search of the perfect appellation for the crown jewel of his luxury powerboats, Carlo Riva drew his inspiration from a suffix that was all the rage in 1962 America: *rama*. The "view of film" had worked its way into the vernacular as "cinerama," and "worldview" was being expressed as

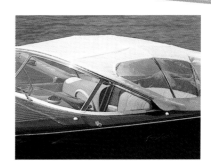

"mondorama." So what did the new Riva line offer its wayfarers? Quite simply, a "view of the water." Hence, Aquarama.

The first of these mahogany masterpieces measured in at 8.02 meters and had two Chris Craft V8 engines of 185 horsepower each. Yet, designer Giorgio Barilani was loath to stop there. Having just created the speedboat equivalent of the lightbulb, he was already working on improvements that would enable Riva to make the jump to light speed.

The next Aquarama model was nearly a quarter of a meter longer and came equipped with V8s of 225 horsepower each. Even with its eight-person "guest list" filled, the Riva could reach speeds of 75 kilometers per hour.

By the mid-1970s, Barilani attained the Everest of speedboat design when he and Carlo introduced the Aquarama Special. Imagine a Rolls-Royce with a Ferrari Dino engine.

This new model was elongated to 8.75 meters to accommodate its ample fuel tanks, enjoyed 350 horsepower per each V8, reached speeds of over 90 kilometers/hour, and came equipped with a "gully which made getting back on board from the bathing ladder easier."

The last word in luxury speedboat development, the Riva Aquarama Special has manufactured 784 different crafts.

107

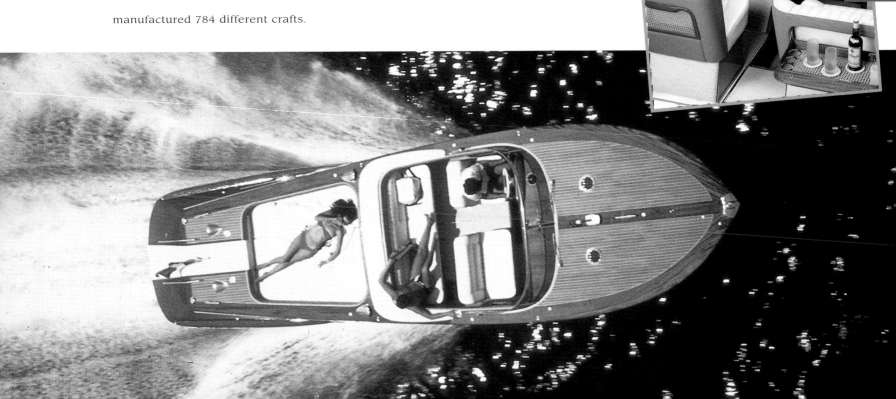

SCHUCO

Since the introduction of the Schuco toy car
into the market in 1912, founder Heinrich
Müller has created a virtual miniaturized history of the automobile.
And what's even more amazing, these Lilliputian
vehicles actually work!

It was Müller's intention to create a toy that precisely mimicked the
construction of the original. Take, for instance, the classic Girato 4000 Mercedes 250 SE.
Prepare to be dazzled.

This particular model features a fully functional four-speed plus reverse H-type
gear box, a working steering wheel, hand brakes, and a sturdy windup mechanism.

Actually, if it weren't for that windup mechanism,
one might begin to think that Schuco was selling the
real McCoy.

In fact, there's no need to wind up the 1937
Command Car. If you want to operate the vehicle...just
whistle. Before you know it, the Command Car will be
moving forward or backward.

Then there's the stunning Turning Car 1010,
which, in case you haven't guessed, turns! Wind it up,

and just as it appears to be flying headlong off the edge of the table, it turns and travels in a more circumspect direction. Throughout its 85-year history, Schuco has been delighting millions of children and car enthusiasts with their craftsmanship and mechanical mastery. But be forewarned: The models do not come preassembled. Therefore, consumers must be prepared to turn their homes into micro-assembly lines. And, by the time manufacturing is complete, they and their cars have achieved an almost mystical oneness. In addition to their classic automobiles, Schuco is renowned for their cuddly little teddy bears, train sets, forklifts, dump trucks, and multifunctional cranes. They even manufacture a line of mini-minivans, just in case families have another "little one" on the way.

SCHWINN

emember your first Celerifere? Who could resist its daring simplicity? A long beam connected to a wheel at each end. Actually, no one born after 1790 ever had one. Instead, most people in the 20th century probably got their two-wheeled start on a Schwinn.

Bicycle development post-Celerifere came slowly, first with the introduction of front-wheel steering in the 1816 Draisine. The stunning pedal breakthrough of 1839 was first seen on the MacMillan, but before anyone could cool his or her jets, the 1855 Velocipede moved its pedals to the front.

The charismatic Ordinary cruised along in 1870, heralding an era of increased speed due to an enlarged front wheel. And finally, the Safety of 1884 switched its pedals to the middle of the frame and added a chain drive. But did the world of personal mobility settle at that?

On a brisk October morning in 1895, German-born engineer Ignaz Schwinn opened the doors to his bicycle factory on the West Side of Chicago. Ignaz and his partner, Adolph Arnold, knew they could do better than the lackluster Safety.

Schwinn took the very best qualities of each of the top bicycles of the time, put his engineering skills to use, and designed the lighter, more durable World Roadster. Although the bike was well received, the bicycle boom of the late 1890s was in full swing and competition was fierce.

From 1895 to 1899, this mode of transportation had gained such rapid acceptance that, seemingly overnight, 300 bicycle factories popped up around the country. They were lean years for Ignaz and Adolph, but just as quickly as the market was flooded, the introduction of the motor car put more than 90 percent of bicycle businesses out to pasture.

Schwinn and Arnold were then left with the best-designed bicycle on the market. By 1900, while most shops were closing their doors, Schwinn was having difficulty keeping up with orders. In fact, they bought out the March-Davis Bicycle Company and moved to a larger factory.

Over the years, Schwinn has dominated the market with innovations such as balloon tires, full-floating saddles, reflectors, fore-wheel brakes, and fender lights. The company created innovative advertising never before seen in the bike industry that captured Americans using their Schwinns in many different ways—for exercise, transportation, travel, work, and freedom to explore. At the same time, the most popular celebrities in America, including Roy Rogers, Bob Hope, Frank Sinatra, Ronald Reagan, Bing Crosby, and Captain Kangaroo, appeared on their Schwinns in ads and promotional materials.

The Schwinn bike was a time machine that captured America's fascinations through the decades, beginning with the Streamline Aerocycle in 1934, the Cycleplane in 1935, the Hollywood in 1937, the Paramount in 1945, the Cruiser in 1955, the Sting Ray and Varsity in the 1960s, and the Apple Krate, Orange Krate, and Manta Ray in the 1970s. Yet it was the classic Black Phantom, introduced in 1949, that set the standard for bicycles and made Schwinn nearly impossible to catch.

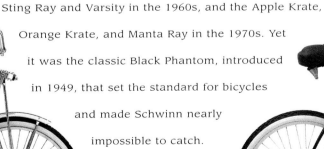

SONY WALKMAN®

"Tune in. Turn on. Tune out." Reading about the introduction of the world's first mini-tape player stereo, one might assume that Timothy Leary was prophetically referring to the Sony Walkman.

It's not known how the Sony Walkman came to hit the streets in 1979. There are two major schools of thought. One involves company chairman Akio Morita requesting that the product development department design a device enabling him to listen to classical music while playing tennis.

The second details Morita's need in the late 1970s for a small, portable music device that would allow him to while away the hours on long transcontinental flights.

Regardless how the Walkman actually came into existence, its emergence resulted in the unheard-of sale of over two million units in its first 18 months. Walkmans became so coveted that no one ever seemed to mind or question the fact that they were purchasing a tape player that couldn't record.

The first Walkman wasn't much of a bargain either, tipping the scales at just over one pound while emptying ones pocket of a whopping $200. And originally, the units weren't even called Walkmans. Those sold in the United States were dubbed Soundabouts, while in the United Kingdom they were known as Stowaway.

Ultimately, Sony, who loosely based their original model on the Pressman Model TCM-100, retained the "man" part of "Pressman" and tacked on their own innovative little prefix.

Although other companies have tried to imitate them, Sony's models are still the most respected. Like fine wine, the Sony Walkman matured with the passing of time and became a mainstay of world culture. Even the *Oxford English Dictionary* in 1986 recognized Walkman as more than just a product by listing it as an actual noun!

In 1987, the very first model, the TPS-L2, entered the hallowed halls of the Smithsonian Institute. And in 1991, Sony recorded the sale of their 40-millionth unit.

STEIFF

In 1892, the Steiff family began creating their soft stuffed bears for *Kinder* throughout Germany. The company fared well and business prospered, but it would be another 10 years before the Steiff Company would break through to the toy industry equivalent of superstardom.

Richard Steiff, nephew of company founder Margarete, came across sketches of a family of bears he'd made at the Stuttgart Zoo. What differentiated these from drawings existent in the design department was Richard's detailing of limb and joint movement. In a scant six months, the Steiff Company came out with its first line of jointed bears.

This cute, cuddly bruin bore the name 55 PB. The number represented its height in a seated position, whereas the *P* stood for "plush" and the *B* for *beweglichkeit* (the German word for jointed...of course). The bear thus named went boffo at the Leipzig Trade Fair in March of 1903.

This first 55 PB—whose fastened limbs were manipulated by strings—sold over 3,000 pieces at a pricey four marks per unit. The following year, a more compact model debuted at the World's Fair in St. Louis, selling 12,000 units. Steiff never looked back.

In 1905, the 35 PAB, affectionately known as Barle, hit the market, sporting joints fashioned out of discs for greater arm, leg, and head mobility, a rounded face, stitched snout, and body filled with excelsior or kapok (wood shavings and silky fibers) for more huggable softness.

The following year, America went bear crazy when *Washington Post* cartoonist Clifford Berryman drew a caricature of President Teddy Roosevelt on a hunting expedition. An adorable bear cub was offered up for Roosevelt to shoot, but the president, horrified, declined to oblige, allowing the cuddly creature to live.

The cartoon became so famous that each ensuing caricature of Teddy Roosevelt included the little cub. Americans, in homage to the president, adopted the plush Steiff Barle bears as their own. By the end of 1906, the term *Teddy Bear* had entered the American vernacular.

STEINWAY

*F*rom Sergey Rachmaninoff, Vladimir Horowitz, and Arthur Rubinstein to Alicia de Larrocha, Emanuel Ax, and Evgeny Kissin, Steinway has been the piano of choice for 90 percent of concert pianists throughout the world. And, in the pop and jazz worlds, Dudley Moore, Billy Joel, and Herbie Hancock have tickled the ivories of those very same Steinway grands.

Emigrating from Seesen, Germany, Heinrich Engelhard Steinweg arrived in Manhattan's Lower East Side in 1850. Bringing along little more than his wife and six of his eight children, Heinrich wasted no time assimilating. Upon

PIANOS

setting foot in the land of opportunity, he immediately reinvented himself as Henry E. Steinway.

Although Henry had worked part time in Germany as a piano maker, he insisted that he and sons Theodore and Henry Jr. start their careers in the New World by hiring on with New York piano manufacturers. It was his belief that they should learn American business practices before embarking on their own venture.

Only two years later, a small loft on Varick Street in New York City became the home of Steinway & Sons. The first pianos to bear the famed surname were typical of instruments of that era. But this ordinariness would be short-lived.

At the New York Crystal Palace Exhibition and Industrial Fair of 1855, Theodore and Henry Jr. created an overlapping string design that allowed "both high and low strings to be longer, more resonant and fuller sounding than any previous pianos." They were unanimously awarded the gold medal.

Word of the Steinway innovation traveled fast, and before the family could celebrate their seventh year in operation, their expanding business forced them to move uptown into a larger space. But this was a mere glint of their brilliance.

They were the first to do away with wood reinforcement and install cast-iron plates, which created greater string tension. Then, in the mid-1870s, the Steinways hit upon a modification that would herald a new era of modern concert grand pianos.

Until that time, pianos tended to be rectangular in shape and not in the "mutton leg" form that is now the norm. It was Theodore who conceived of a continuous, bent rim fashioned out of $18^3/_{16}$-inch-thick layers of maple wood. This design, when coupled with Steinway's overlapping string construct and cast-iron reinforcement, produced a volume and tonal quality that, to this day, remains unrivaled.

STETSON

W hat can you do with $100, a small rented room, a few tools, and $10 worth of fur? You can start up a nice little enterprise just like John B. Stetson did in 1865.

Acutally, the story picks up a few years prior to Mr. Stetson setting up shop. John had ventured out West with a few of his compadres, and one night, while sitting around the campfire, he wowed them with little more than a piece of fur. He wet it, kneaded it, stuck it in boiling water, then kneaded it some more, and before anyone could say "Draw!" that piece of fur up and turned into felt.

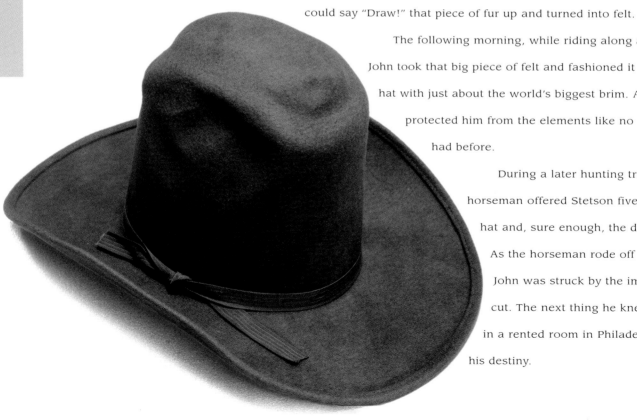

The following morning, while riding along a hot, dusty trail, John took that big piece of felt and fashioned it into an enormous hat with just about the world's biggest brim. And that hat protected him from the elements like no other ever had before.

During a later hunting trip, a fellow horseman offered Stetson five bucks for his hat and, sure enough, the deal was done. As the horseman rode off into the sunset, John was struck by the image the man cut. The next thing he knew, John was in a rented room in Philadelphia, fulfilling his destiny.

Hats worn by those heading west had, up until that time, run the gamut from Civil War castoffs to tams to top hats to derbies. Never had anyone set forth to make a specific type of hat to protect riders from the sun, wind, and other elements. So when Stetson hit the market with his first line of Boss of the Plains hats, needless to say, the country clamored for this new invention.

Stetson was having trouble keeping up with the demand. The accessory even sparked a whole new slew of expressions such as "Keep it under your hat." The hats were so big they offered a surefire safe place to store treasures and vital information.

Then came the 10-gallon hat. Although the Stetson weaves were so tight one could carry water in them, the 10-gallon was really only good for a few quarts. In fact, according to William Reynolds and Ritch Rand's *The Cowboy Hat Book*, the term "10-gallon" derives from the Spanish system for measuring the width of sombrero hatbands.

Today, there exists a lot of competition in the cowboy hat business, but here are just a few folks who wouldn't be caught anywhere without their Stetsons: Buffalo Bill Cody, Ronald Reagan, Gene Autry, Jimmy Stewart, Henry Fonda, Tom Mix, Walter Brennan...and "the Duke," John Wayne.

STEWART SURFBOARDS

These days, when we hear talk of "surfing," our minds conjure up visions of Bill Gates facing a monitor, shredding digital peelers down the information superhighway. But we're talking real surfing here, where you strap a longboard to your woody, cruise past the little old lady from Pasadena, and head for the coast.

When they founded their company, husband-and-wife team Bill and Chris Stewart began revolutionizing the world of longboard surfing. It was the late 1970s, and Bill had gained a reputation as one of the best—if not the best—airbrush artist in the industry.

He'd spent several years honing his craft at the legendary Hobie Surfboards of Dana Point. Under the tutelage of Rick James, Bill not only perfected his airbrushing expertise, but he also studied the fine art of surfboard design. It wasn't long before Bill—ever the restless, venturesome spirit— sensed he was "tip riding" what could be a pretty rad trend.

121

In 1979, he and Chris set up their very first Stewart Surfboards shop in Laguna Beach, California. The time had come to wipe out the competition. Experimenting with new rocker, rail, and bottom concepts, Stewart longboards quickly gained the respect of noseriders, goofy foots, and scoot 'n' shooters throughout the world.

Legends such as Phil Edwards, Hobie Alter, Herbie and Christian Fletcher, Mickey Muñoz, Geoff Moysa, John Moritz, Colin McPhillips, Ted Robinson, Jeff Kramer, and Henry Ford not only swear by Bill's longboards but also have joined the Stewart team. Nothing like having the best in the business designing your boards.

Now based out of San Clemente, California, Stewart Surfboards has become the largest-selling manufacturer of longboards in the world. They've been immortalized on the TV cult hits *Baywatch* and *Beverly Hills 90210*, as well as in song—that's Bill shaping a board in Jimmy Buffett's "Mexico."

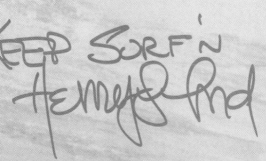

KEEP SURF'N
Henry Ford

SWISS ARMY KNIFE

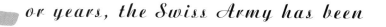

*F*or years, the Swiss Army has been holding the world at bay, tirelessly protecting Switzerland's borders armed with little more than a zealous love of country and an unrivaled courageousness. But from where does this bravery stem? Quite simply, from the knowledge that in their pockets, they possess the last word in weaponry: the Swiss Army Knife.

It was back in 1886 that the Swiss Army first issued a folding knife to each of their fighting boys. Minimalist and simple, the knife offered nothing more than a blade that one might rely on for self-protection. No toothpicks, no tweezers, no nail file.

Three years later, the Army developed a rifle that needed to be dismantled by men in the field. One catch: The disassembly required a screwdriver. A call immediately went out to the Swiss cutlery industry to develop a folding knife that also contained the aforementioned screwdriver, plus a can opener and a reamer.

Unfortunately, Swiss manufacturers were incapable of mass production at the time. Not so for a factory based in Solingen, Germany. They rose to the occasion and fulfilled the Army's wishes. Not long after, however, a Swiss company named Victorinox developed the necessary machinery, and all knife production returned to Switzerland.

At roughly the same time, Theodore Wenger, a Swiss minister spending time in the United States, decided to return home to his wife. Upon his reentry, he was hired as general manager by a company that had just won a contract from the Army to produce knives. Interestingly, this company was not Victorinox.

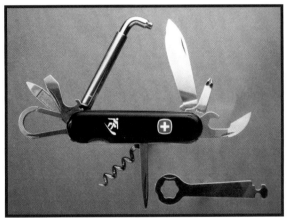

While on the job, Wenger had the foresight to acquire a manufacturer of spoons and forks. He then combined all efforts into a factory called Fabrique Suisse de Courtetellerie located in Services. Not long after, Wenger purchased Fabrique Suisse and renamed the company Wenger et Cie.

Although Wenger can boast of having created the "genuine Swiss Army Knife," the Victorinox Company continues to supply similar knives to the Army. In fact, competition became so fierce that in 1908 the Swiss government intervened and, like William Tell, whose crossbow is symbolized on each knife, split the contracts right down the middle.

The domain of the Swiss Army Knife now reaches far beyond Swiss borders. With models such as the Wenger Mountain Bike, the Wenger Toolchest Plus, and the Wenger In-Line Skate, there is a perfect tool for any occasion.

KNIVES

TROJAN® CONDOMS

To gain a more heightened appreciation of condoms, it's helpful to parse the actual word, thereby analyzing its basic components. First we have *con*, from the Latin *con*, meaning "with." Next we have *dom*, from the Old English suffix *dom*, meaning "dignity" or, in some instances, "jurisdiction." So where does that leave us? With *condom* meaning "with dignity, power, control, authority."

Nobody knows whether this has any bearing whatsoever on the etymology of the word. Condoms appear to have been around since ancient times. Hieroglyphics indicate that the highly advanced Egyptians were the first to practice safe sex. Greco-Roman culture later adopted the device for disease prevention, contraception, and, at various bacchanals, as decoration.

These early prophylactics were fashioned out of thin, flexible animal intestines. It wasn't until the 16th century that

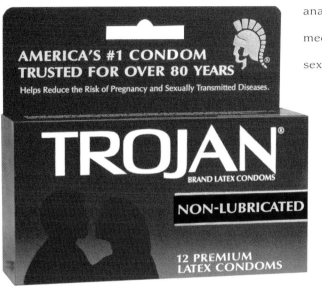

anatomist Gabriello Fallopius invented medicated sheaths for protection against sexually transmitted diseases.

The advent of vulcanization in the 19th century introduced the era of the rubber condom. A major breakthrough in the history of the product came in the 1930s with the development of latex. This innovation decreased thickness while increasing durability and disease protection.

Carter Products, a company at the forefront of condom manufacture, was one of the first to jump on the latex bandwagon with their Trojan brand. Again, one is left to speculate why Carter chose the name.

Historically, Trojan warriors have been associated with tremendous strength and staying power, attributes also associated with Carter's products. America agrees, for Trojan accounts for 50 percent of all U.S. retail sales.

Today, with the threat of HIV transmission, latex condoms are scientifically demonstrated to be the only form of contraception, aside from abstinence, through which the AIDS virus most likely cannot be transmitted.

TUPPERWARE®

Tupperware® brand products.

A virtual icon of Americana.

Timeless in form, eternal in function.

This paragon was created in 1946 by plastics innovator Earl Tupper who, until that time, had devoted his entire inventory to the World War II effort. In fact, Earl's plastics were probably first used in the production of the gas masks American GIs used on the battlefields of Europe.

When the war ended, the late sixties were just a glimmer in America's eyes, and Dustin Hoffman's character was a solid 20 years away from receiving the monosyllabic "plastics" counsel in *The Graduate*. But Earl didn't wait that long.

In search of a market for his sturdy yet lightweight and flexible plastic he dubbed Poly-T, Earl targeted the American zeitgeist of the mid- to late 1940s. It was time to cash in on the genesis of the baby boom.

Fathers came home from battle and mothers returned from aiding the war effort to focus on reestablishing the nuclear family. This was a family that would spend considerable time at home, dining together in the comfort of a neat and tidy kitchen.

Enter Tupperware. Contrary to what one might think, its entrance into the marketplace received a tepid response. Nevertheless, Earl Tupper did not retreat. Instead, he advanced, topping off his product with a unique feature.

In 1947, fashioning the seals after paint containers, Earl hit upon the virtually "airtight seal," still in wide use today. Homemakers now had the luxury of keeping food fresh well beyond their wildest imaginings.

Yet, initially, sales far from skyrocketed. Evidently, the problem housewives were having was that "they needed demonstrations in order to understand how it worked." Hence, the very first Tupperware Home Party was held in 1948.

Such was the success of its Home Parties that Tupperware was immediately removed from retail outlet shelves. Thus, Tupperware would become one of the world's leading direct sellers, with $1.4 billion in global net sales in more than 100 countries.

VESPA

"Sembra una vespa!"

(Translation: "It looks like a wasp!") With these words, Enrico Piaggio named the most successful scooter of all time, with a total of 15 million sold worldwide. As president of his company, he had this prerogative (however spontaneously it was administered), and thus Vespa the vehicle was thereafter called—in favor of its initial designation—"Paperino," or "Donald Duck" (presumably for the sound it emitted).

Enrico Piaggio has been compared with Henry Ford in his adoption of mass individual transport to postwar Italy. In 1945, he owned a fighter airplane factory whose prospects—not to mention those for Italy itself—appeared bleak. Piaggio's solution to the poverty and devastation he saw around him was to come up with a cheap form of

transportation that was easy to operate and simple to build.

Piaggio hired a talented engineer, helicopter pioneer Corrado d'Ascanio, onto the project. Although D'Ascanio himself disliked motorcycles, in a matter of weeks, he triumphantly unveiled the Vespa's now-familiar design.

At first, sales were slower than the vehicles themselves. Folks harbored suspicions about the Vespa's small wheels and its somewhat precarious sense of balance. Yet, while a mere 2,500 models sold in 1945, within 10 years, sales had jumped 100 percent. One reason for this stunning turnaround: At the time, one could operate the vehicle without bothering to obtain a license.

Factories soon sprouted up in France, Belgium, Spain, Germany, Brazil, and India. An international network of Vespa enthusiasts was born as Vespa Clubs, complete with competitions and congresses, sprang up the world over.

The movie world, too, went wild for the Vespa—not surprisingly, given its sleek, seductive mystique. John Wayne, Henry Fonda, and Jean-Paul Belmondo all posed on their scooters in an early nod to product placement. In the sublimely romantic *Roman Holiday*, Audrey Hepburn and Gregory Peck share a climactic, carefree drive through the aforementioned city on none other than a Vespa.

Other companies invariably competed with Piaggio for the market share, only to have annual sales rarely squeak above 100,000 units. But Vespa has not merely captured the market; it has also won nine gold medals in sporting events. For the record, the 1951 prototype of the 125 was clocked at a speed of 171 kilometers/hour.

Vespa expeditions have ventured as far as Tokyo, Australia, the Congo, and, yes, the North Pole. The roller has even been spotted in New York's Museum of Modern Art.

129

SCOOTERS

VOLKSWAGEN BEETLE

t was January 17, 1934, when a German former electrical engineer turned car designer decided that the time was nigh for a utilitarian vehicle. The designer's name was Ferdinand Porsche, who was later to gain notoriety for having created his namesake vehicle.

Newly elected Nazi leader Adolf Hitler received Dr. Porsche's proposal and told the Reichsverband der Automobilindustrie (RDA, the German Motor Industry Association) to give him the green light. They did so...reluctantly.

The problem was that Germany was experiencing an era of heightened entitlement at the time, and the idea of an economical, unpretentious vehicle did not exactly fit the RDA's lofty vision. So, somewhat handcuffed by strict guidelines, Dr. Porsche set to work.

Greatly influenced by the reliability and accessibility of the Model-T, Porsche wanted to create a vehicle the average citizen could afford—transportation for the masses. It was 1935, and an estimated one out of 49 Germans actually owned a car.

C A R S

After several months, in October 1935, the first "People's Car" or "Volkswagen" prototype was built. It was thought to be a remarkable breakthrough in small car design, with full-steel bodywork, comfortable seating for five, and heating—a feature not even standard in luxury cars of the day. It also had the nifty quirk of carrying its engine in the rear. (This was simply for concentrating the weight over the back axle.)

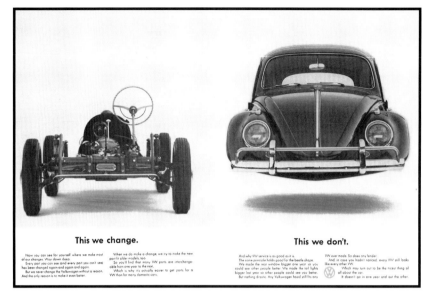

This we change.

This we don't.

The following year, two more prototypes were constructed, but the RDA—fearing pressure from private car manufacturers who were less than thrilled with the competition—shelved the designs.

After a brief stint in Detroit, Porsche suggested certain modifications to the initial prototype, and on May 28, 1938, production got the go-ahead. Less than a month and a half later, the first VW "People's Car" rolled off the assembly line.

The cars were immediately well received, and Hitler enthusiastically renamed them the "Strength Through Joy Car." Much to his chagrin, the name did not stick, for on July 3, 1938, the *New York Times* printed an article about this new car, remarking that it resembled a beetle.

In 1949, Dutch importer Ben Pon brought the Beetle to the United States, where it was displayed at the German Industrial Exhibition in New York. However, the success of the car was not immediate. VW of America was founded in 1955, and more than 20,000 Beetles were imported. By 1965, annual sales of the "Bug"—as it came to be known in the United States—reached 500,000. Its lack of styling and pretense made the Beetle a symbol of the late-1960s counterculture.

Although no longer made in Wolfsburg, Germany, but in Brazil and Mexico, Dr. Porsche's creation has sold over 20 million, making it the most successful car in history. Not bad for an automobile the Ford Company dismissed as not being "worth a damn."

See? No springs.

WARJNG

In 1936, President Franklin Roosevelt offered the United States a New Deal, Jesse Owens redefined track and field, King George V bid England adieu, and Fred Waring introduced the world to his brand-new invention...the blender.

Actually, the true inventor of the blender was a Mr. Frederick J. Osius, who termed his creation "a disintegrating mixer for producing fluent substances." In truth, the device didn't work all that well. But that didn't stop Mr. Osius, who believed so devoutly in his gadget that he camped out backstage at New York's Vanderbilt Theater, awaiting famed American bandleader Fred Waring, following the latter's radio broadcast. When Waring appeared with his bandmates, Mr. Osius announced that he held "the key to a revolution in food processing," and persuaded Waring to invest in his invention.

Six months and $25,000 later, the team of Osius and Waring weren't much better off than they were that fateful summer of '36. Major problems still existed with the mechanism, which caused Waring to turn development over to his partner, Ed Lee. In addition, he hired German designer Peter Muller-Munk, who gave the processor its now-famous Art Deco motif.

The item was dubbed the Miracle Mixer, and in September of 1937, it hit the streets for the then-exorbitant price of $29.95.

The Miracle Mixer didn't exactly fly off shelves, nor did it do any of its proposed revolutionizing. The following year, the item was renamed the Waring Blender in an effort to capitalize on the fame of its prime investor. In fact, wherever Fred Waring and his band played, music lovers were apt to experience what may very well have been America's first infomercials.

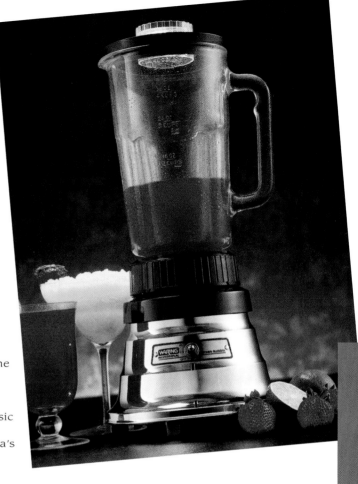

In his dressing room, Mr. Waring would demonstrate the blender's attributes as he mixed daiquiris and other assorted tropical blends. The ever-popular Rudy Vallee was so smitten with his colleague's side project that he himself took to promoting the item.

In 1943, war restrictions brought production to a halt, and shortly thereafter, Fred Waring sold the company, having moved exactly 86,705 units. A man by the name of Hazard Reeves took over and, much to Waring's dismay, sold over a million blenders in the ensuing 10 years.

And not long after, a Dr. Jonas Salk would prepare culture materials integral to the development of his polio vaccine with the aid of none other than a Waring Aseptic Dispersal Blender.

WINCHESTER

Plunking down a good deal of his hard-

earned money, Oliver Winchester made his very first investment

in the munitions industry in 1855. The company was called Volcanic

Repeating Handguns, and although they relocated and changed their

name to the New Haven Arms Company the following year, this marks

the humble beginnings of what became known as "The American Legend."

By 1866, Winchester had built up enough capital to purchase the outfit outright and change its name to the Winchester Repeating Arms Company. That same year saw the introduction of the first gun to bear the Winchester name, model 1866, AKA Yellow Boy.

Winchester's reputation for excellence, which quickly spread along the Eastern seaboard, paralleled America's growing lust for westward expansion. The forty-niners may have paved the way for millions of others, but the West was indeed wild, and to venture forth into this wilderness without the reliability of a Winchester was, to put it mildly, unwise.

Oliver himself passed away in 1880, shortly after giving birth to his legacy. The company carried on the tradition, most notably with the

Winchester 94. This model, introduced in 1894, quickly became a favorite with deer hunters and earned the moniker "The Gun That Won the West."

Perhaps the greatest endorsement the company ever received was from frontier legend Buffalo Bill Cody, who swore by his Winchester, as did every single member of his Wild West Show, including Annie Oakley. Dime novels related fictional accounts of Buffalo Bill brandishing his Winchester as he brought countless "bad guys" to justice.

The romantic figure of the rugged Western hero that Cody cut had such an overwhelming impact that none other than Teddy Roosevelt himself soon owned several Winchesters. Can't you just picture him, Winchester in hand, charging up San Juan Hill, yelling (what else?), "Bully!"

135

MODEL 94
1884 · 1994

ZEISS BINOCULARS

In 1854, a young officer in the Italian Army by the name of Ignaz Porro began experimenting with what would eventually become known as prism binoculars. Porro was dissatisfied with the limits of outdated hand-held telescopes, which had been around since the 17th century.

These devices were too long, often clumsy, and seldom accurate—not the kinds of attributes that lend themselves to longevity. Porro's initial work involved the combination of two telescopes for greater depth distinction, and although he documented his activities, he worked on his own and was never able to perfect the apparatus.

Nearly 20 years later, an entrepreneur named Carl Zeiss was operating a successful mechanical and optical workshop in Oberhausen, Germany. One of Zeiss' employees was physicist and mathematician Ernst Abbe.

Professor Abbe had begun working on an optical system that closely and inadvertently mirrored the work of Ignaz Porro.

In 1873, Abbe came up with his prism erector system, but the Zeiss company delayed production. Such things, one must trust, happen for a reason.

For renowned chemist and glass engineer Otto Schott would later team with Abbe, and it was his innovation in glass design that helped bring Abbe's invention to fruition. In 1894, the Zeiss company went into full-scale production on their very first line of binocular telescopes.

By August of that same year, word of Carl Zeiss' accomplishment spread far and wide. Even His Majesty Kaiser Wilhelm II placed an order for a "10x shear-jointed telescope."

Then, in 1902, Roald Amundsen bought a pair of Zeiss field glasses, which he carried along as he set out in 1924 on his fateful journey to the North Pole. Grand Admiral Togo purchased his binoculars in 1904, and so relied on them that his statue in Yokosuka depicts him sporting a pair.

Other Zeiss devotees have been Albert Einstein and that laconic leader of the Lost Generation, Ernest Hemingway. During his war correspondent years, Papa relied on his Zeiss to help magnify details that later found their way into his classic prose.

ZIPPO

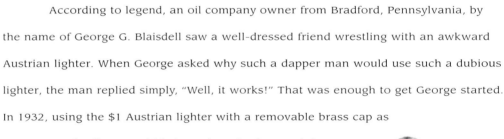

Whether they're lighting the Marlboro Man's cigarette or upstaging Arnold Schwarzenegger as he delivered his blistering "Hasta la vista, baby," Zippo lighters have found their way into the hands of some of the 20th century's greatest icons.

138

According to legend, an oil company owner from Bradford, Pennsylvania, by the name of George G. Blaisdell saw a well-dressed friend wrestling with an awkward Austrian lighter. When George asked why such a dapper man would use such a dubious lighter, the man replied simply, "Well, it works!" That was enough to get George started. In 1932, using the $1 Austrian lighter with a removable brass cap as a prototype, he fine-tuned his invention—he fastened the cap with an external hinge, squared off the edges, and reduced its size by a quarter of an inch.

This new design, coupled with the pre-existing feature of a "wind hood" that surrounded and "windproofed" the wick, would soon become America's coveted smoking companion.

Success, however, was not automatic for Blaisdell. After carefully selecting a name for his

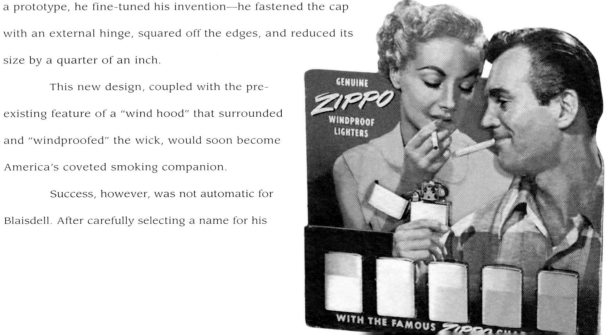

creation, which owed a great deal to another invention that was quickly taking the country by storm—the dazzling and enigmatic zipper— George saw his Zippo falter in its initial sales.

Racking up a disappointing $62.15 in its first month from the sale of a scant 82 lighters, the company attempted myriad ad campaigns that yielded little to no return. Not until the outbreak of World War II did Zippo lighters become fully entrenched in the hearts and minds of our fighting boys.

Blaisdell decided to make his lighters available only through military post-exchanges. And with an astounding 95 percent of all U.S. servicemen listed as smokers, Zippos soon became a necessary part of every GI's uniform.

With a ringing endorsement from famed wartime correspondent Ernie Pyle and backed by numerous stories of soldiers whose lives were saved when their Zippos stopped round after round of bullets, Zippos were assured their place in history.

Legend also holds that the first all-out attack on the Japanese mainland was signaled on the USS *Cabot* by the flash of a Zippo.

Now in its 65th year of existence, Zippo has slightly improved upon its humble origins. In 1996, the company recorded the sale of their 300-millionth lighter.

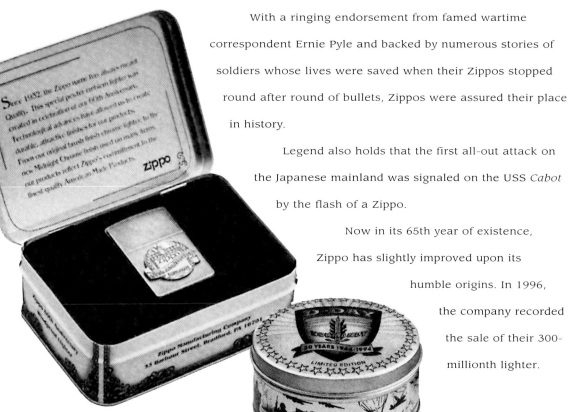

CLASSICS Registry

Abel Automatics

165 Aviador Street

Camarillo, CA 93010

800-848-7335

Alpha Industries Inc.

1600 Spring Hill Road

Vienna, VA 22182

703-506-2482

American Express

Executive Offices

American Express Tower

World Financial Center

New York, NY 10285

800-528-4800

G.H. Bass & Co.

600 Sable Oaks Drive

P.O. Box 9431

South Portland, ME 04116-9431

207-791-4000

Bausch & Lomb

One Bausch & Lomb Place

Rochester, NY 14604-2701

716-338-6000

(Ray-Ban sunglasses)

Bayer Corporation

100 Bayer Road

Pittsburgh, PA 15205

412-777-2000

Buck Knives

1900 Wells Boulevard

El Cajon, CA 92020

619-449-1100

Burberrys Limited

9 East 57th Street

New York, NY 10022

800-284-8480

Callaway Golf

2285 Rutherford Road

Carlsbad, CA 92008-8815

619-931-1771

Campbell Soup Co.

Campbell Place

Camden, NJ 08103

800-909-7687

Cantieri Riva s.p.a.

24067 Sarnico

Italy

01139-35-91-02-02

Carter-Wallace Products

1345 Avenue of the Americas

New York, NY 10105

800-984-1777

(Trojan® condoms)

Chanel

9 West 57th Street

New York, NY 10019

800-550-0005

(for catalog and stores)

Chrysler Corporation

1000 Chrysler Drive

Auburn Hills, MI 48326-2766

248-576-5741

(Jeep® Wrangler)

Coca-Cola Company

Coca-Cola Plaza

Atlanta, GA 30301

800-438-2653

The Coleman Company, Inc.

3600 North Hydraulic

Wichita, KS 67219

800-835-3278

Converse Inc.

One Fordham Road

North Reading, MA 01864-2680

800-428-2667

Deere & Company

John Deere Road

Moline, IL 61265

888-669-7767

Dutch Gold Honey, Inc.

2220 Dutch Gold Drive

Lancaster, PA 17601-1997

717-393-1716

A.W. Faber-Castell GmbH & Co.

Nuernbererstr 2

D-90546 Stein

Germany

01149-911-9965-0

Filofax Inc.

Building 101

Merritt 7 Corporate Park

Norwalk, CT 06851

800-345-6798

Gibson Guitars

1818 Elm Hill Pike

Nashville, TN 37210

800-444-2766

Haribo GmbH & Co. KG

Postfach 1720

D-53007 Bonn

Germany

01149-228-537-0

Harley-Davidson Motor Company

3700 West Juneau Avenue

P.O. Box 653

Milwaukee, WI 53201

414-342-4680

HATCO

601 Marion Drive

Garland, TX 75042

800-325-2662

(Stetson Hats)

H.J. Heinz Company

P.O. Box 57

Pittsburgh, PA 15230-0057

412-237-5740

Hermés

745 5th Avenue

New York, NY 10151

800-441-4488

Hillerich & Bradsby

P.O. Box 35700

Louisville, KY 40202

502-585-5226

(Louisville Slugger)

Hohner, Inc.

P.O. Box 15035

Richmond, VA 23227-0435

804-550-2700

International Watch Company

Baumgartenstrasse 15

CH - 8201 Schaffhausen

Switzerland

01141-53-28-55-55

Lacoste

Devanlay US Inc.

551 Madison Avenue

New York, NY 10022

800-4-LACOSTE

Ralph Lauren Fragrances

Division of Cosmair, Inc.

575 5th Avenue

New York, NY 10017-2450

212-818-1500

Leatherman Tool Group, Inc.

P.O. Box 20595

Portland, OR 97294-0595

503-253-7826

Leica Camera Inc.

156 Ludlow Avenue

Northvale, NJ 07647

201-767-7500

Levi Strauss & Co.

800-USA-LEVI

(for catalog and stores)

Lionel LLC

26750 23 Mile Road

Chesterfield, MI 48051-2493

810-949-4100

Louis Vuitton

130 East 59th Street

New York, NY 10022

800-285-2255

(for catalog and stores)

Lucchese Boots

6601 Montana

El Paso, TX 79925

800-637-6888

Manischewitz Co.

1 Manischewitz Plaza

Jersey City, NJ 07302

201-333-3700

Martini

In every good bar.

Mattel Inc.

333 Continental Boulevard

El Segundo, CA 90245-5012

800-524-8697

Michelin® North America, Inc.

P.O. Box 19001

Greenville, SC 29602-9001

864-458-5000

Mont Blanc Inc.

75 North Street

Bloomsbury, NJ 08804

800-388-4810

Monte Cristo

Cuban cigars,

not available in

the United States

Nabisco Inc.

7 Campus Drive

Parsippany, NJ 07054

800-622-4726

(Barnum's Animal Crackers

and Oreo Cookies)

Perrier Group of America

777 West Putnam Avenue

Greenwich, CT 06830

800-937-2002

PEZ® Candy, Inc.

35 Prindle Hill Road

Orange, CT 06477

203-795-0531

Polaroid Corporation

549 Technology Square

Cambridge, MA 02139

617-386-2000

Precise International

15 Corporate Drive

Orangeburg, NY 10962-2625

914-365-3500

(Swiss Army Knife)

The Procter & Gamble Company

1 Procter & Gamble Plaza

Cincinnati, OH 45202-3315

513-983-1100

(Ivory Soap)

Schuco® GmbH & Co.

Kreulstr. 40

D - 90408 Nuernberg

Germany

01149-911-93-55-15-0

142

Schwinn Cycling & Fitness Co. Inc.

1690 38th Street

Boulder, CO 80301-2602

800-SCHWINN

Sony Electronics Inc.

1 Sony Drive

Park Ridge, NJ 07656-8003

800-222-7669

Steiff USA

31 East 28th Street

New York, NY 10016

212-779-2582

Steinway & Sons

One Steinway Place

Long Island City, NY 11105

800-366-1853

Stewart Surfboards

2102 South El Camino Real

San Clemente, CA 92672

714-492-1085

Tupperware Corporation

P.O. Box 2353

Orlando, FL 32802-2353

800-858-7221

Vespa

OFRAG Vertriebsgesellschaft

Ruetistrasse 19

Ch - 8952 Schlieren

01141-1-730-11-66

Volkswagen of America Inc.

3800 Hamlin Road

Auburn Hills, MI 48326

248-340-5000

Waring Products Division

283 Main Street

New Hartford, CT 06057

800-492-7464

Winchester Rifles and Shotguns

U.S. Repeating Arms Company, Inc.

275 Winchester Avenue

Morgan, UT 84050-9333

801-876-3440

Harry Winston, Inc.

718 Fifth Avenue

New York, NY 10019

212-245-2000

Wolverine World Wide, Inc.

9341 Courtland Drive

Rockford, MI 49351

616-866-5500

800-422-HUSH

(Hush Puppies®)

Wurlitzer

235 Moonachie Road

Moonachie, NJ 07074

800-987-5480

Carl Zeiss

D-73446 Oberkochen

Germany

01149-7364-20-0

Zippo Manufacturing Company

33 Barbour Street

Bradford, PA 16701

814-368-2700

CLASSICS Photo Credits

6–7: Abel fishing reel images courtesy of Abel Automatics.

8–9: Alpha flight jacket images courtesy of Alpha Industries Inc.

10–11: American Express Card images courtesy of American Express Company.

12–13: BARBIE® dolls © 1997 Mattel, Inc. All rights reserved. Used with permission. Photographs courtesy of Mattel, Inc.

14–15: Barnum's Animal Cracker image (page 14, upper right) courtesy of Nabisco Inc. Remaining photographs by Nina Prommer.

16–17: Bass Weejuns photographs courtesy of G.H. Bass & Co.

18–19: Bayer Aspirin images courtesy of Bayer Corporation and Golin/Harris Communications.

20–21: Buck Knife images courtesy of Buck Knives and Venture.

22–23: Burberry raincoat images courtesy of Burberrys Limited.

24–25: Callaway golf club images courtesy of Callaway Golf.

26–27: Campbell's soup images courtesy of the Campbell Soup Company.

28–29: Chanel No. 5 photographs by Nina Prommer.

30–31: Coca-Cola images and trademark courtesy of The Coca-Cola Company.

32–33: Coleman lantern images courtesy of The Coleman Company, Inc.

34–35: Converse All Star images (page 34 and page 35, middle left) courtesy of Converse Inc. Remaining photographs by Nina Prommer.

36–37: Faber-Castell pencil images courtesy of A.W. Faber-Castell GmbH & Co.

38–39: Filofax images courtesy of Richartz & Fliss Inc.

40–41: Gibson guitar images courtesy of the Gibson Guitar Company.

42–43: Haribo Gummi Bear images courtesy of Haribo GmbH & Co. KG.

44–45: Harley-Davidson photographs courtesy of the Harley-Davidson Motor Company Archives. All rights reserved. Copyright © H-D Michigan, Inc.

46–47: Harry Winston diamond jewelry images courtesy of Harry Winston, Inc.

48–49: Heinz ketchup images courtesy of H.J. Heinz Company.

50–51: Hermès Kelly bag images courtesy of Hermès.

52–53: Hohner harmonica images courtesy of Hohner, Inc.

54–55: Honey Bear photographs by Nina Prommer.

56–57: Hush Puppies® shoes photographs courtesy of J. Walter Thompson Company.

58–59: I.W.C. images courtesy of International Watch Company.

60–61: Ivory soap image (page 60, lower left) copyright © The Procter & Gamble Company, used with permission of The Procter & Gamble Company. Remaining photographs by Nina Prommer and Kurt Wahlner.

62–63: All Jeep® vehicles images are used courtesy of Chrysler Corporation.

64–65: John Deere tractor images courtesy of Deere & Company.

66–67: Jukebox images courtesy of Wurlitzer.

68–69: Lacoste images courtesy of Lacoste/Devanlay US Inc.

70–71: Leatherman tool images courtesy of Leatherman Tool Group, Inc.

72–73: Leica camera images courtesy of Leica Camera Inc.

74–75: Levi's® jeans photographs by Nina Prommer.

76–77: Lionel train images courtesy of Lionel LLC.

78–79: Louisville Slugger photographs by Nina Prommer.

80–81: Louis Vuitton luggage images courtesy of Louis Vuitton.

82–83: Lucchese boot images courtesy of Lucchese Boots.

84–85: Manischewitz image (page 84, upper left) courtesy of Manischewitz Co. Remaining photographs by Nina Prommer.

86–87: Martini photographs by Kurt Wahlner.

88–89: The Michelin® baby ad and other images are used with permission of Michelin North America, Inc. All rights reserved.

90–91: Montblanc pen images courtesy of Nike Communications.

92–93: Montecristo cigar photographs by Nina Prommer and Kurt Wahlner.

94–95: Oreo cookie images courtesy of Nabisco Inc.

96–97: Perrier images courtesy of Perrier Group of America.

98–99: PEZ® candy images courtesy of PEZ® Candy, Inc.

100–101: Polaroid image (page 100) courtesy of Polaroid Corporate Archives. Remaining photographs by Kurt Wahlner.

102–103: Polo by Ralph Lauren images courtesy of Ralph Lauren Fragrances.

104–105: Ray-Ban sunglasses images courtesy of Bausch & Lomb, Ray-Ban Eyewear Division.

106–107: Riva Aquarama speedboat images courtesy of Cantieri Riva s.p.a.

108–109: Schuco® toy images courtesy of Schuco® GmbH & Co.

110–111: Schwinn bicycle images courtesy of Schwinn Cycling & Fitness Inc.

112–113: All images of the Sony Walkman® stereo cassette player courtesy of Sony Electronics, Inc.

114–115: Steiff teddy bear images courtesy of Rea Lubar.

116–117: Steinway piano images courtesy of Steinway & Sons.

118–119: Stetson cowboy hat photographs by Kurt Wahlner.

120–121: Stewart surfboard images courtesy of Stewart Surfboards.

122–123: Swiss Army Knife images courtesy of Dunwoodie Communications, Inc.

124–125: Trojan® condom images (page 124, upper left and page 125, upper left) courtesy of Carter Products and Ruder Finn Public Relations. Remaining photographs by Nina Prommer.

126–127: Tupperware® brand product images courtesy of Tupperware Corporation.

128–129: Vespa images courtesy of Vespa.

130–131: Volkswagen image (page 30) courtesy of the Detroit Public Library National Automotive History Collection. Remaining photographs courtesy of Volkswagen of America.

132–133: Waring blender images courtesy of Waring Products Division/Dynamics Corporation of America.

134–135: Winchester handgun images courtesy of U.S. Repeating Arms Company, Inc., trademark courtesy of Winchester.

136–137: Zeiss binoculars images courtesy of Carl Zeiss.

138–139: Zippo lighter images courtesy of Zippo Manufacturing Company.